Irish History

ISBN 0-75258-225-9 (Hardback)

This is a Parragon Publishing Book
This edition published in 2002
Parragon Publishing
Queen Street House
4 Queen Street
Bath BA1 1HE, UK

Copyright © 1999 Parragon

Printed in Indonesia
Created and produced by
Foundry Design & Production

Cover design by Blackjacks

Irish History

Séamas Mac Annaidh

p

Contents

Contents

Introduction

The island of Ireland lies within sight of mainland Britain, but although their histories have been intertwined for many centuries, they remain very different places. The Romans saw Ireland ('Hibernia') as a cold inhospitable place, yet the Vikings found it well worth the sail across hundreds of miles of treacherous seas, first to plunder and later to settle. The Normans, descendants from the Norsemen who settled in what is now called France, saw Ireland as an extension of their growing kingdom, but it was a part that they could not easily hold on to as they became 'more Irish than the Irish themselves' (see p.73) and the core of their own civilisation fragmented – other Normans became English or French and they waged war against one another.

▲ *Vikings raided Ireland in the eighth and ninth centuries*

▲ *St Patrick, the patron saint of Ireland*

Successive English rulers sought to dominate or to cajole the Irish nature, seeing Ireland as a colony to be plundered or as an almost integral part of their kingdom. Yet it was never to become assimilated as part of England, nor to be treated in the same way. One suspects that the Westminster government would have reacted in a different manner had the Great Famine been taking place in Yorkshire rather than across the Irish Sea. Down through the years, those who sought to gain from Ireland often found that it merely presented them with further problems. Ireland was a neighbour that just could not be ignored and any gains made there did not come cheaply.

Ireland, with one of the oldest cultures and vernacular literatures in Western Europe, was a country the English never fully understood. It was a wild place, full of magic and superstition according to their chroniclers, and yet, at the same time, it was renowned across continental Europe for its piety and learning – as a land of scholars and saints – no less.

▲ *Seamus Heaney, winner of the Nobel Prize for Literature*   ▶ *Irish hero, Finn McCool*

▲ *Pub musicians playing traditional music*

This Ireland presents many faces, loving, teasing, inscrutable, wise, frivolous and fanatical. From the heroes of the Celtic myths to the starving victims of the Great Famine, from St Colm Cille to Seamus Heaney, this is the Ireland of one hundred thousand faces, all different, and each of them with a story to tell.

Language and lore have always been central to Irish life. One of the preliminary tales to the great epic, the *Tain Bo Cuailgne*, tells of how the poets – the keepers of Ireland's lore – came together deliberately to try to reconstruct the story from the different sections that each of them could remember so that the epic could be recovered and preserved in its entirety. This happened long before the *Tain* was first written down in the eighth century by Christian monks who shared this same passion for language, learning and lore that brought about a fusion between the bardic and the Christian schools, and created something very powerful which has lasted in different forms down to the present day.

Ireland's impact on world culture has been disproportionate to its size. Seamus Heaney's Nobel Prize for Literature is one of the latest examples of how the literary traditions of Ireland, in all their various guises and in both Irish and English, continue to flourish.

Few European countries have changed as much as Ireland in the last decades of the twentieth century. Confidence and prosperity are buzz-words of the new Celtic Tiger economy. The 150-year-old tide of emigration has been stemmed and turned. Irish people coming home are joined by English and Americans, and by continental Europeans who see Ireland as a good place to live, to work and to raise a family.

The old and the new exist side by side with startling effects. One is as likely to hear Irish spoken in a trendy Dublin club as in a small village pub. In the west of Ireland, there are thatched cottages with satellite dishes.

Young people – who make up the majority of the population – are redefining what it means to be Irish, to be Europeans as they approach the new millennium. It is clear that most of them like what they are. Well-educated, upwardly and outwardly mobile, they find their icons among the new generation of Irish film and rock stars who can take their place beside the best the world has produced.

This small island with a population of only 5.5 million has recently become the hub for many multinational hi-tech industries. Ireland may not have coal or minerals in abundance, but its greatest natural resource is this young population, which is bright friendly and enthusiastic.

Even in the north-east, those six contentious counties of Northern Ireland, it seems that the clouds of despair have begun to lift and to clear. There is hope and optimism where previously there was none.

Nobody can tell what tomorrow may bring, but the people of Ireland have many reasons to be hopeful about the future.

▲ *An unemployment march during the 1930's Depression*   ▶ *Copies of the Stormont Agreement*

THE
AGREEMENT
THIS AGREEMENT IS ABOUT <u>YOUR</u> FUTURE.
PLEASE READ IT CAREFULLY.

It's Your Decision

Mesolithic Peoples in Ireland

The modern Irish landscape is still dotted with many Stone-Age monuments. These are almost the only remnants of the earliest civilisations, which archeologists tell us came in separate waves, the earliest around 9000 BC.

These Mesolithic, or middle Stone Age, people lived mostly in the northern half of the island and had probably crossed over from what are now known as Scotland and Wales, as the coast of Ireland can be seen from both these places. They lived in small groups, often near the rivers and coasts, leading short, unsettled lives and surviving mainly as hunter-gatherers in a landscape that was quite different from the landscape of today.

Ireland at that time was so densely covered in forest that some scientists believe the Great Irish Elk (*megaloceras giganteus*), which became extinct about 10,000 BC, died out because its large antlers kept getting caught up in the branches of trees. The earliest Irish settlement that has been found is at Mount Sandel, on the bank of the river Bann near Coleraine. It dates from 7000–6500 BC.

The earliest known human sites in Ireland are almost 9,000 years old and are littered with thousands of stone edges, used as we would use knives or scissors. Microliths were set into wood in rows to produce a longer and consequently more effective cutting edge. Nobody knows who these people were, but they may have been of the hunter-gatherer type and ranged through much of the north-east. Evidence of these people has been found near Coleraine, Dundalk, the Shannon basin at Boora, County Offaly and as far south as the Blackwater.

▲ *Stone Age monument*

Neolithic Ireland

By 3000 BC, Mesolithic man had been superseded by the more advanced Neolithic, or new Stone Age man, whose origins were in continental Europe. They led a much more settled life, rearing livestock, clearing and cultivating the soil.

At the Ceide Fields, near Ballycastle in north County Mayo, a network of new stone-age fields has recently been discovered under 6 m (20 ft) of bog, indicating that there was once a large population in this area which is now quite remote.

Neolithic peoples were also responsible for the construction of the great megalithic passage grave at Newgrange, County Meath. This tomb, which today stands 11 m (36 ft) high and has a diameter of 85 m (280½ ft), is the work of a large disciplined society. Similar monuments found at nearby Knowth and Dowth leave little doubt that there was a major population

▲ 'Triskele' motif carved inside the tomb at Newgrange

centre here in the valley of the Boyne river. The Newgrange tomb also reveals that these people had an interest in astronomy, for a small opening at one end of the 19-m (63-ft) passage allows sunlight to illuminate the central chamber at the heart of the mound at dawn on the winter solstice.

Archeologists believe that this spectacular ancient tomb was built about 5,000 years ago (3200 BC), 500 years before the pyramids in Egypt and 1,000 years before Stonehenge. Newgrange is now said to be one of the world's oldest structural sites.

▲ *Passage grave on the hill of Tara, County Meath*

Early Myths and Legends

Another, parallel, version of the early history of Ireland comes from the *Book of Invasions*, a collection of myths, legends and beliefs gathered together by Christian historians around AD 1100, although it is clearly part of a much earlier tradition.

▲ *Basalt 'columns' near the Giant's Causeway*

THIS COLLECTION TELLS of giants, of supernatural peoples, of great battles, of sorcerers, of gods and magic spells. It gives the Irish a genealogy that dates back to Noah – via Spain, Egypt and Babel – and tells how a people known as the 'Milesians' conquered Ireland and banished such tribes as the *Fir Bolg* and the *Tuatha De Danann*. The Milesians are reputedly the ancestors of the people now known as Irish. Another feature of many of the Irish legends is *dinnseanchas*, or 'lore of place', in which the storyteller tries to explain how a particular place received its name or how a certain geographical feature was formed. It is through *dinnseanchas* that the volcanic basalt columns of the north Antrim coast have acquired the name, the Giant's Causeway.

The Causeway was the work of the giant Finn McCool (see p.31), an Ulster warrior and commander (or king) of Ireland's armies. Legend has it that Finn could pick thorns out of his heels while running and was capable of amazing feats of strength. Once, during a fight with a Scottish giant, he scooped up a huge clod of earth and flung it at his fleeing rival. The clod fell into the sea and turned into the Isle of Man. The hole it left filled up with water and became Lough Neagh.

Irish history is rich with such myths and legends. Many weave true history with brilliant threads of myth and lore; this happened with the legend of St Patrick, patron saint of Ireland. The old stories of Irish kings are woven and intertwined with tales of faeries and mystical gods. Add to these the Irish Druids, the Celts and the birth of Christianity, and the line between fact and fantasy dims even more.

Book illustration showing Finn McCool and Princess Tasha ▶

The Irish Bronze Age

By 2000 BC, people had begun to mix copper and tin to make bronze tools and weapons. The Bronze Age people have also left many monuments as testimony to their time in Ireland.

IRELAND'S BRONZE AGE lasted until about 500 BC, when the country was colonised by the Celts. One of the characteristic features of this era is dolmens. These comprise three upright stones with a flat capstone balanced on top to form the central chamber of a grave mound. Over the centuries, the earth around many of these dolmens became eroded and the stones were exposed; today they stand starkly against the skyline. Dolmens appear to have been constructed both for single burials and as cemeteries (as appears to have been the case at Knowth and Dowth). Similar dolmens can also be found in Cornwall and Brittany.

▼ *Ancient funeral showing a dolmen grave entrance*

During this time, throughout Europe, Asia and the Far East, horns, trumpets and bells were made using bronze. Around the Mediterranean, sheet bronze was riveted to form large light horns, while further north in Ireland and northern Europe horns were cast in clay moulds. Of all the Bronze Age instruments that survive in the world, Ireland, with 104 horns and 48 bells has by far the largest amount – representing more than half the total. These unique instruments have been carefully studied and today they are being manufactured and played in Ireland once more.

Over hundreds of years many attempts were made to play the 104 horns that survive from the Irish Bronze Age. All were met with failure due to the large 'single cavity' mouthpiece which is a feature of the bronze horn family. Indeed, one of the most exciting musical discoveries of the twentieth century was the rediscovery of how to play the Bronze Age horns of Ireland, Scotland and England.

▲ *Exposed dolmen on a limestone plateau in County Clare*

The Celts and their European Origins

The Celts were an Iron Age people who originated in central Europe and who reached Ireland about 500 BC. They also went as far west as Spain and as far east as Asia Minor. Their language and culture became so dominant that little evidence remains of the society of their predecessors.

THEIR IMPLEMENTS, ORNAMENTS and weapons from this period show a strong northern European influence. Archeological evidence suggests that there were several separate influxes of Celts into Ireland between 500 BC and AD 500. These are known as the

▼ *The Gundestrup Cauldron, showing distinct celtic iconography*

Hallstadt and La Tène civilisations, the former from an early site found in Austria, the latter from a more advanced site found in Switzerland. The La Tène Celtic influence is found in Ireland from around 200 BC.

The area known as Gaul includes all of modern France, Belgium and most of Switzerland. It is a land of great topographic, climatic and archeological diversity, a diversity reflected in its strongly marked regionalism, even today. Although the word Gaul equates with Keltoi or Celt, all of Gaul was not Celtic: there were Iberians in the south-west, Ligurians all along the Mediterranean coast, Greeks at Marseilles, and Germans scattered along the middle and lower Rhine. In Gaul, as in Italy and elsewhere, the distinction between Celtic and non-Celtic is blurred.

The east of Gaul was most in contact with the La Tène 'heartland', where there were wagon burials of 'princely' type, associated with large hill forts, such as the burial of the lady of Vix, at the foot of Mont Lassois hill fort. Vix is only one of a number of important grave mounds; there was a neighbouring one at Sainte Colombe, which also contained imported luxury bronze 'grave-goods'.

◀ *A celtic statue*

Celtic Languages

'Celtic' is a linguistic term (pronounced with a hard 'c') which describes a group of languages nowadays represented by Irish, Scots Gaelic and Manx, which belong to the 'q' Celtic group, and Welsh, Breton and Cornish, which make up the 'p' Celtic group.

THE 'Q' CELTS COULD NOT pronounce 'p' and so either dropped it completely (*pater* in Latin, meaning 'father', is *athair* in modern Irish) or changed it to a 'q' type sound, thus *purpura* in Latin, meaning 'purple', is *corcora* in Irish.

Speakers of Irish can understand Scots Gaelic without much difficulty, but will not be able to understand Welsh or Breton at all, as the two groups of languages have been developing separately for over 2,000 years.

The Celtic insular languages are mostly those spoken on the islands, typically Britain, Ireland, Man and part of France. The Insular languages are divided into two branches, the Goidelic and the Brythonic. Manx is a form of Gaelic spoken on the

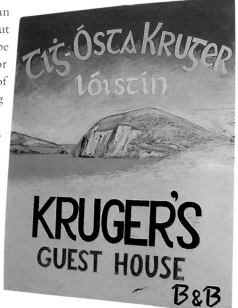

A bilingual sign ▶

Isle of Man. The last native speaker of Manx died in 1974, but many are learning the language today, and recordings exist of native speakers. There are many native speakers of both Irish and Scottish Gaelic today, not only in Ireland and Scotland, but also in Nova Scotia, in Canada. Language became central to the culture of the Irish, much more so than other Celtic races. It was, and is, a source of great pride and identity.

Note: Modern Ireland has only four provinces, Ulster, Munster, Leinster and Connacht. Meath was the fifth and *cuige*, the Irish word for province, retains this tradition – *cuig* means five.

▲ *Irish road sign*

Ogham, the Celtic Alphabet

What we know about the early Celts derives from accounts of them on the Continent written by Greek and Roman historians, as the Celts themselves did not leave any written records other than a number of inscriptions on standing stones, most of which mark graves.

THEY HAD A PRIMITIVE alphabet known as *ogam* or *ogham*, which comprised a series of notches cut into the edge of a stone. Using a method such as this, each stone could record little more than the name of the person buried beneath it.

▼ *Small bronze animal figures, including a bronze celtic rabbit*

The word *ogham* has been used to refer to:

- An alphabet of 25 characters used for stone and wood inscriptions in Celtic Ireland and Britain.
- A group of 20 sacred trees that give names to the letters of the *ogham* alphabet.
- A calendar of 13 months named for some of the trees.
- A purported system of hand-signing used by Druids that relates to the alphabet.
- A system of divination in Celtic paganism that may or may not relate to the alphabet.

The word *ogham* comes from the phrase *beth luis nion,* in the same way that the word 'alphabet', comes from the names of the first and second letters of the Greek language. The letters consist of one to five perpendicular or angled strokes, meeting or crossing a centre line. The form of the letters allows them to be carved easily on objects of wood or stone, with the edge forming the centre line. Most *ogham* inscriptions come from Ireland and Scotland.

▲ *Intricately carved celtic cross*

St Patrick

St Patrick's mission to Ireland appears to have lasted about 30 years and its impact was immense. AD 432 is the date traditionally given for the start of his mission. It is probable that there was a small number of Christians in the country before this time, as Ireland had considerable trading links with both Roman Britain and continental Europe.

THE IRISH ALSO raided and plundered their neighbouring territories, and it was during one such raid that the young Patrick, the son of a Christian Roman official, was taken captive and brought back to Ireland where he was to spend the next six years tending sheep in a remote area.

During his captivity, he had time to consider his faith. As a result, when he eventually escaped and made it back to his home and family – we do not know exactly where – he was

▲ *St Patrick*

haunted by a vision of the Irish people calling to him, saying, 'we ask thee, boy, come and walk among us once more'.

Patrick is most famous throughout the world for reputedly having driven all the snakes out of Ireland. Different tales tell of his standing upon a hill, using a wooden staff to drive the serpents into the sea, banishing them forever from the shores of Ireland.

One legend says that one old serpent resisted, but the saint overcame it by cunning. He is said to have made a box and invited the reptile to enter. The snake insisted the box was too small and the discussion became very heated. Finally the snake

▲ *Stained glass window in honour of St Patrick*

entered the box to prove he was right, whereupon St Patrick slammed down the lid and cast the box into the sea.

It is true there are no snakes in Ireland, but the chances are that there never have been since the time the island was separated from the rest of the continent at the end of the ice age. As in many old pagan religions serpent symbols were common, and possibly even worshipped. Driving the snakes from Ireland was probably symbolic of putting an end to pagan practices.

Information about Patrick comes from his own *Confession* (written in an untutored Latin). This is the earliest Irish historical document and also appears to be the first historical document in Ireland not written in *ogham*. So not only is St Patrick's *Confession* the only contemporary narrative telling of the arrival of Christianity to Ireland, it also marks the beginning of documented history, a history that was to be developed and sustained by the monastic church for the next 1,000 years.

▲ *St Patrick spent his early life as a shepherd*

Book illustration from the history of Finn McCool ▶

The Merging of Pagan and Christian Ireland

Folklore links the pre-Christian and Christian periods very neatly in the story of Oisin in *Tir na nOg*, the Land of Eternal Youth. Oisin was one of a group of legendary heroes called the *Fianna* (from whom the Fenians of the 1860s took their name), who were led by the larger-than-life figure of Finn McCool (*Fionn mac Cumhail*), sometimes a giant, sometimes a warrior, sometimes a figure of fun.

OISIN FELL IN LOVE with the beautiful Niamh, who led him away to *Tir na nOg*, where he remained for many years. Eventually he became homesick and she granted him permission to return – on condition that he remained on his magical horse at all times and did not set foot on the soil of Ireland. On his return, however, Oisin discovered to hi sdismay that several hundred years had passed: all the legendary heroes known to him were dead and forgotten and a new discipline, Christianity, was now in vogue. However, before Oisin had time to return to Niamh in *Tir na nOg*, disaster befell him. He stopped to help a man who was trying to lift a large stone; as he strained with the rock the strap of his saddle broke and he fell to the ground, instantly becoming a very feeble old man.

As Oisin lay dying, St Patrick passed by. The two great men began to talk, discussing the relative merits of their respective civilisations. This story was faithfully recorded by the monks, thereby consigning the heroic era of the Celts to history and marking the triumph of the new, Christian, era. St Patrick himself became a legendary figure and a large number of sites, especially in Ulster, Leinster and Connacht, are associated with him. One legend tells of how he used the shamrock, a plant with three leaves on one stem, to explain the mystery of the Holy Trinity: the three leaves represented the three persons in one God, the Father, Son and Holy Ghost. This is why the shamrock has become a symbol so closely associated with Ireland.

No one can agree from which plant St Patrick picked the shamrock: the small, yellow-flowering hop clover (*Trifolium procumbens*); a variety of white clover (*Trifolium repens*); or the black medic (*Medicago lupulina*). These plants are native to Europe and naturalised in North America. The European wood sorrel (*Oxalis acetosella*), which grows in both Europe and Asia, is also often considered to be the true shamrock.

Statue of St Patrick at Slane Friary ▶

The Synod of Druim Ceat

Not long after the spread of Christianity, a great monastic movement began. Although the early Christian Church, from which Patrick came, was Episcopal, that is, having bishops and diocese in an echo of Roman civil structures, the Irish Church was to develop in a unique way.

THE MONASTERY WAS to become Ireland's central unit of administration, this was probably because of the structure of Irish society where the *tuath* was the unit of administration.

These *tuaths* were often controlled by family groups. The same came to be true of the monasteries. For instance, 10 of the first dozen abbots of Iona belonged to the same family as its founder, St Colm Cille. Often these monasteries developed because of the strong personalities of their founders, many of whom are still revered today as saints; among them Brendan of Clonfert, Brigid of Kildare, Ciaran of Clonmacnoise, Colm Cille of Derry and Iona, Kevin of Glendalough and Jarlath of Tuam

St Mary's Cathedral in Limerick is one of the earliest places of Christian worship in

◄ *A celtic cross on the holy island of Iona, in Scotland*

Ireland. The current building dates back to 1168. The chancel arch, which marks the entrance to the sanctuary, is strikingly composed of six semi-circular concentric and recessed arches. This impressive example of Hiberno-Romanesque architecture is justly famous and many visitors still flock to this place of worship every year.

Soon, many of the most important churches were under the control of the monasteries rather than the bishops. Even at Armagh, where the bishop was seen as the direct successor to St Patrick, by the eighth century the abbot was in charge and the bishop was a subordinate member of his community.

▼ *St Colm Cille, who travelled from Ireland to Iona to preach Christianity*

St Brigid of Kildare

One of the most significant of the early Irish saints, St Brigid soon became known as 'Mary of the Irish'. Many myths, legends and miracles are associated with her and she is also revered in Brittany.

ST BRIGID IS one of Ireland's patron saints. On her feast day, 1 February, people make 'St Brigid's Crosses' from rushes. She is a good example of the significant role played by women in the early Celtic church.

Irish monasteries and covents were unlike the great stone-built buildings of continental Europe. The earliest examples were made mostly of wood and wattles and consisted of a church and a collection of huts within an enclosure, not unlike the *raths* that ordinary people lived in.

The monks or nuns worked as communities, growing food and praising God. However, as well as working the monastery or convent lands

▼ *St Brigid's Cathedral, Kildare, which dates back to* AD *480*

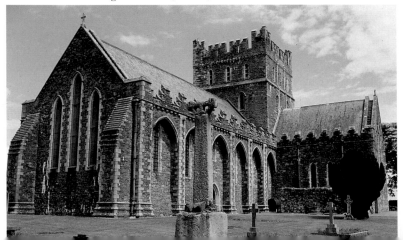

and enduring the strictures of the religious life, they also cultivated learning. Both the scriptures and secular literature were studied in great detail and much time was devoted by monks to the meticulous copying of manuscripts of these texts.

In the early centuries of Christian Ireland, a remarkable fusion of native Irish learning and Latin literacy took place. Pre-Christian Ireland had its learned men, keepers of the Brehon Laws, poets and storytellers of the highest order. Their period of training was every bit as rigorous and exacting as that undergone by the prospective clerics of the monastic schools, not least because the entire body of their tradition had to be learned off by heart.

▲ *Stained glass window, at Loughrea Cathedral, depicting St Brigid and St Brendan*

St Colm Cille's Missions

With Christianity flourishing in Ireland it is not surprising that missionaries began to take their teachings to other shores. The first and most significant of these was Colm Cille, who, with Brigid and Patrick, is one of the three patron saints of Ireland.

H E WAS BORN in Gartan, County Donegal, and founded monasteries at Derry, Swords, Durrow and Kells. He secretly made a copy of a psalter belonging to St Finnian of Moville, his old teacher, who, when he discovered what had happened, demanded the return of the copy.

Their dispute was taken to the High King, who made what is regarded as the world's first copyright ruling: 'to every cow belongs its calf, to every book its copy.' In anger, Colm Cille raised an army against the king but was defeated. Over 3,000 were killed and, at a church synod held in AD 563, it was decreed that he should leave Ireland forever and convert as many souls as had been killed in the battle. Exile was regarded as the equivalent of martyrdom.

St Colm Cille ▶

With 12 companions, he sailed to Iona and founded a monastery, which became the hub of a group of monasteries in Scotland, the north of England and Ireland that were highly significant in the development of Christianity. This was especially true in Scotland, where Colm Cille is known as St Columba.

His Irish name means 'dove of the church', and a Latin psalter, the *Cathach*, probably the oldest surviving manuscript in Ireland, may even be the contentious copy he made of St Finnian's book. Iona was the most famous of Colm Cille's monasteries. Here some of the most important records of early Ireland were compiled and, given the northern origins of St Colm Cille and his followers, it is not surprising that the emphasis is on the northern half of the country.

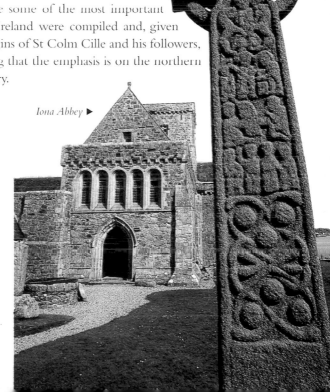

Iona Abbey ▶

The Irish in Europe

A generation later, St Columbanus, inspired by St Colm Cille's example, travelled across Europe, founding monasteries as he went. The last of these was erected in Bobbio, northern Italy, in AD 613.

THUS, EVEN AS the pagan tribes of northern Europe were still rampaging across the continent, the Christianity, learning and Latin-based literacy that had been nurtured in the relative peace and tranquillity of Ireland was replanted among the ruins of the Roman Empire.

Not only did the Irish import books and copy them in their monasteries, but they took them with them wherever they went. An important library was established at Bobbio soon after the monastery was founded by Columbanus and, because of this two-way traffic in manuscripts, some very important early Irish texts and historical documents, which would probably have been lost had they remained in Ireland, have survived in continental libraries.

Columbanus was the founder of several European monasteries. He had left Ireland, at the invitation of King Childebert of Burgundy, to establish a monastery at Annegray. He also founded monasteries at Luxovium (Luxeuil) and at Fountaines. He left Burgundy to preach to the Allemani of Switzerland.

His monasteries were known for the strictness of their rules (which the Benedictines later ameliorated) and their emphasis on corporal punishment. In addition to his rule for monks, Columbanus wrote a penitence and poems.

The network of Irish-founded monasteries in mainland Europe meant that Ireland could no longer be regarded as an isolated and uncivilised island on the edge of the known world, as it had appeared to the Romans. The European dimension would remain significant for the next 1,000 years and would become particularly important again in the sixteenth and seventeenth centuries, when Irish society and civilisation faced its greatest challenges.

◄ *An illustration from the* Book of Kells, *lovingly created by monks*

Viking Invasions

The Vikings, aristocratic Scandinavians, were great sailors and ruthless warriors who travelled in well-built longships. They began to raid the coasts of Ireland, Britain and France in the AD 790s. The island-based monasteries were particularly vulnerable to attack and made rewarding targets for the fast-moving raiders.

THIS RANDOM RAIDING persisted for several decades, gradually intensifying until it became a concerted campaign by the end of the AD 830s, by which time the Vikings had established bases at Annagassan in County Louth and, more importantly, at Dublin.

▼ *Viking boats raided Ireland for many decades*

Then, however, just when it seemed as though they were on the point of overrunning the country, several of the Irish kings managed to hit back at them and contain the threat. The crisis subsided and the Vikings withdrew to consolidate their positions at Dublin, Wexford, Waterford, and Youghal.

These Viking settlements merged into the mosaic of small kingdoms that covered Ireland. They played their part in the regular local power struggles until, in AD 914, the arrival of a huge Viking fleet in Waterford marked the start of a new campaign. The Vikings attacked Munster and Leinster, defeated the Ui Neills and their allies who had marched southwards against them, and greatly consolidated their position.

The Viking age in Ireland ended early in the eleventh century. During the first phase, the Vikings generally raided Irish monasteries and returned to Scandinavia with their booty. They took part in internal Irish wars and made Ireland a centre of European trad. They also introduced the use of money and had a great influence on art, language, folklore   and
place names.

▲ *A Viking silver lion*

The Viking City of Dublin

Much new information about the Viking city of Dublin came to light in the 1970s during a major building project at Wood Quay, alongside the River Liffey. It is now clear that the Vikings had a considerable impact on the structure of the Irish economy.

THEY INTRODUCED THE use of coinage and greatly increased the volume of overseas trade using their fast, well-built boats. The towns they built – which were centres of craft and commerce – were to become a permanent feature of Irish society.

Dublin is truly a Viking city. It is so called from *Dubh Linn* – which translates to mean 'Black Pool'. Dublin's area of Baldoyle is also an integral part of Viking Ireland: no physical evidence of Scandinavian presence has been uncovered here, but the historical connections of Baldoyle with the Vikings are well documented. The name itself, Baldoyle or *Baile Dubh Ghaill*, means the 'town of the dark foreigners'. The Vikings established settlements built on or near river estuaries (such as Dublin, Wexford and Waterford). This was because they could sail up the rivers to the hinterland (surrounding areas) and because towns on estuaries or high ground could be more easily defended.

They laid the foundations for a thriving medieval city – a city with thick walls, many towers and gates – parts of which can still be seen. The Viking rulers built two great cathedrals here, Christchurch and St Patrick's (of which the famous Jonathan Swift, author of *Gulliver's Travels*, was dean). Dublin Castle, also dating from this time, has been rebuilt as a

Georgian Palace. These buildings still play their part in the life of the city.

Over the following centuries, Dublin evolved into an important city, welcoming Dutch, Huguenot, English and Jewish immigrants, all of whom contributed greatly to its growth.

▲ *St Patrick's Cathedral, Dublin*

The Normans

At the same time that the Vikings were aiming to annex Ireland, they were also attacking France. By *c.* AD 900, they had ravaged northern France to such an extent that there was little plunder to be found along the rivers that had formed their major avenue of attack. A Danish army, led by Hrolf, arrived in AD 911 to pillage the lower Seine Valley, leaving a lasting impact.

HROLF ATTEMPTED TO besiege Chartres without success, but his army was such a threat to the Seine valley, that Charles, king of the Franks, negotiated a treaty at St Clair-sur-Epte. Under this treaty all the land bounded by the rivers Brestle, Epte, Avre and Dives was granted to the Danes; effectively the land they already controlled. By AD 924 the Franks were forced to grant the Danes the districts of Bayeux, Exmes and Sees, and, in AD 933, the Cotenin and Avranchin.

Within two generations, Hrolf (who was baptised in AD 912 and re-named Rollo) and his followers had adopted the Franks' language, religion, laws, customs, political organisation and methods of warfare. They had become Franks in all but name, for they were now known as Normans, men of Normandy – the land of the Nordmanni or Northmen.

The Normans' love of the sea and their dynamism led to commercial prosperity; in later years they were to establish strong links with Ireland. By the middle of the eleventh century, Normandy was extremely powerful. Desire for conquest, in conjunction with limited available land, led many Normans to travel abroad in pursuit of military

A Viking ship off the coast of Normandy ▶

goals: to Spain to fight the Moors; to Byzantium to fight the Turks; to Sicily in 1061 to fight the Saracens; and, of course, to England in 1066.

Battles Against the Vikings

The most successful Viking settlements were all in the southern half of Ireland. However, in the latter half of the tenth century, a new Irish dynasty came to prominence in Munster. They captured the Viking city of Limerick and in time came to be headed by Brian Boru (*Boroimhe*) (AD 941–1014).

AT THE SAME TIME, Mael Sechnaill, who became king of Tara (Meath) and defeated the Norsemen in the Battle of Tara in AD 980, proceeded to lay siege to Dublin, which he soon captured.

The rise of these two men, representing the northern and southern dynasties respectively, led to conflict as they both sought to extend their sphere of influence. Brian triumphed in 1002 when Mael Sechnaill submitted to him without a fight at Tara. He was then able to proclaim himself emperor of the Irish. Brian was not without opposition; Ireland had never previously had a supreme king, though many had claimed the title of *ard-ri*, or High King.

▲ *A map showing Ireland at the time of the Viking battles*

In Leinster, the king, Mael Morda, joined forces with the Norsemen of Dublin and sought overseas aid from other Viking colonies in a struggle which culminated in a last desperate confrontation at Clontarf on Good Friday 1014. In the bloody battle that ensued the Irish emerged victorious, but their leader Brian was slain. Thus the Battle of Clontarf (see p. 48) effectively marked the end of two eras: the reign of terror of the Vikings and the reign of the first true king of all Ireland.

▲ *A stone bearing Viking carvings*

Brian Boru and the Battle of Clontarf

Brian Boru (*Boroimhe*) was probably born in County Clare. He used his position as King of Munster to gradually gain control of the southern half of Ireland.

ONCE HE HAD captured Dublin, he was able to use its men and military resources to advance his campaign to be recognised as king of Ireland. By 1002, he had succeeded well enough to describe himself as 'Emperor of the Irish' in a hand-written addition to the *Book of Armagh*, a manuscript compiled at Armagh in AD 807–808, which contains a copy of the New Testament and other texts, including a copy of *St Patrick's Confession*.

He destroyed the dominance of the Ui Neills in the northern half of the country. By 1011, he was truly king of the whole island. This lasted for only three years, ended by the Battle of Clontarf in 1014. Despite beating the Scandinavian forces, Brian was slain by a retreating Viking as he rested in his tent. Popular belief claims that he was on his knees saying his Good Friday prayers and giving thanks for the victory when hacked to death. Brian's son and heir also died in the battle.

The Ostmen (Norsemen) were thereafter considered subordinate to the kings of Ireland, and were no longer regarded as a military threat. They were relegated to their cities in Dublin, Waterford, Limerick, Wexford and Cork, and it was only in these places that they were able to retain some degree of autonomy. After a time, so many Norsemen had married Gaels, that, in effect, they became Gaels themselves.

Brian Boru after the Battle of Clontarf ▶

The Struggle for Supremacy

It has been said that only 20 or so Vikings escaped the Battle of Clontarf alive. Although the High King Brian Boru lost his life in the battle, the Carroll, or *Cianachts,* displayed great bravery under his leadership.

AFTER THE DEATH OF Brian Boru, there was a great deal of strife, as various minor kings and their supporters sought to gain the position he had held. He was succeeded by his main rival, Mael Sechnaill, king of Tara, who ruled until 1022.

In the period that followed his death, eight kings claimed the supremacy, including three belonging to the house of Brian Boru, two of the Ui Neills and two of the O'Connors of Connacht. This shows that initially no single dynasty was strong enough to become dominant. The two O'Connors, Turlough and his son Rory, appeared to be on the point of forming a feudal–style hereditary kingship, similar to that found in neighbouring countries at that time. Dermot (Diarmaid) MacMurrough, the king of Leinster, however, had other plans (see p.54).

Around this time, the church was going through a process of renewal and regeneration. The supremacy of the Bishop of Armagh had been acknowledged by Brian Boru during his lifetime and after the king's death his body was brought to Armagh and buried there – an act which acknowledged both the importance of the king and of Armagh itself. In 1111, the Bishop of Armagh presided over a national synod held near Cashel, another important ecclesiastical seat. At this synod, the first attempt was made to divide Ireland up into diocese.

▼ *Armagh Cathedral*

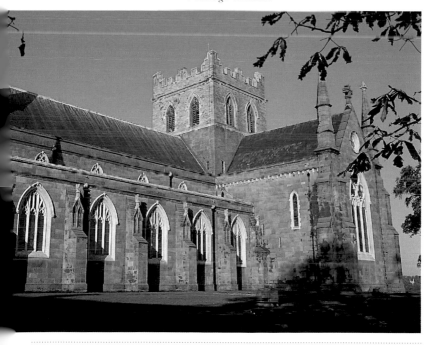

Dermot MacMurrough

Dermot MacMurrough, king of Leinster, abducted the wife of O'Rourke, king of Breifne, in 1152. He kept her for a year. O'Rourke waited until 1166 until an opportunity for revenge presented itself.

MACMURROUGH'S POWER-BASE in Leinster had weakened over the years and his most powerful allies were now dead. O'Rourke, now supported by various north Leinster factions moved against MacMurrough from the north and the Norsemen of Wexford prepared to attack him from the south. His situation was hopeless, his base in Ferns was taken and his palace sacked.

When O'Rourke destroyed his last lands in Ferns, MacMurrough sailed with some of his loyal followers. It was 1166. He landed at Bristol, and from there he went to look for King Henry II of England, who was currently at war with the French; he finally found him at Aquitane.

This was not the first time Henry had considered an Invasion of

▼ *Clough Castle, built in Norman times*

Ireland and with MacMurrough now requesting assistance, he did not want to waste the opportunity. Henry was unable to start another war at present, but to keep MacMurrough as a friend he did a number of things: he accepted his fealty, promised help, and gave him gifts.

Journeying through Wales and Pembrokeshire, MacMurrough secured the aid of others, these included FitzHenry, Carew, FitzGerald, Barry, Prendergast, Fleming, Roche, Cheever and Synott. Having gathered this support, MacMurrough sailed for Ireland, in 1167. He did recover Ferns, but was soon attacked by his old enemy, O'Rourke, as well as O'Connor – he was forced to submit, and ended up giving O'Rourke gold for past damages.

▲ *Henry II agreeing to help Dermot MacMurrough*

Henry II and Strongbow

Henry II, a vigorous and shrewd leader, realised that he personally was too heavily involved in other territorial campaigns to lead an expedition to Ireland at that time, but he also realised that the support of the King of Leinster could prove useful in the future. He accepted MacMurrough's pledges of loyalty and in return gave him a letter inviting his subjects to assist the King of Leinster.

ON LEAVING FRANCE, MacMurrough sought the assistance of Richard Fitzgilbert de Clare, a powerful Norman leader in Wales. Known as 'Strongbow', he drove a hard bargain. Yes, he would lead an expedition to Ireland that would restore Dermot MacMurrough to power but on condition that he could marry Aoife, the king's eldest daughter, and that the right of succession in Leinster would pass to him and his heirs.

There was a small unsuccessful landing in 1167 which briefly restored MacMurrough to power (see p. 55) but the main Norman

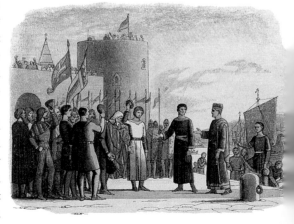

▲ *Henry II being greeted by his subjects*

attack began in 1169 (after MacMurrough's defeat) with a landing at Bannow Bay. The archers and knights were joined by MacMurrough's forces and together they marched on the Norse city of Wexford.

Unprepared for the new type of warfare practised by the Normans, the Norse offered little resistance and the following day the town surrendered. O'Rourke and O'Connor marched against their old adversary and after some fighting near Ferns an agreement was reached. MacMurrough was to be king of Leinster south of Dublin and his foreign allies were to leave the country. O'Connor was content that his supremacy as High King had been recognised, but he failed to realise that the Normans still posed a significant threat.

MacMurrough then wrote to Strongbow, assuring him that the ground had been well prepared.

▼ *Kilkenny Castle, built by 'Strongbow' in 1172*

The Fall of Dublin and Waterford

Strongbow sent a small advance guard of less than 100. They dug in on the Wexford coast and a large force of Irish and Norse marched against them from Waterford. Before the Irish had time to regroup, the Normans burst forth and the Irish were routed.

SUBSEQUENTLY, STRONGBOW and his army landed and joined forces with the advance party. Together they marched on Waterford and took the city. After the marriage of Strongbow and Aoife, the Normans marched on Dublin. It wasn't long before the city was in their hands.

On returning to Dublin, Strongbow now found the city under siege from a large Irish army, supported at sea by the Norse. The Irish were taken by surprise when the Normans attacked while O'Connor and many of his men were bathing in the River Liffey. This led to the siege being lifted – the Normans had achieved a significant victory over both the Irish and the Norse.

▼ *The coastline of Wexford Bay at sunset*

These events had not gone unnoticed in France where King Henry II suddenly realised that if Strongbow were to establish a strong independent kingdom in Ireland, this could be a threat to his own supremacy. He landed at Waterford in October 1171 with a strong force of soldiers and marched up through the country, where the Normans, the Norse and the Irish had little choice but to submit to him.

The conquest of the northern part of the country was begun by John de Courcy (see p. 60), who, with about 300 knights from the Dublin garrison, captured Downpatrick, capital of the ancient kingdom of Ulidia from which the province of Ulster gets its name.

Portrait of Henry II ▶

John de Courcy in East Ulster

John de Courcy (c.1150–1219) came to Ireland with Henry II. Having captured Downpatrick and repulsed repeated attempts by the Irish, he used it as a base for the next 27 years.

UNDER HIM, THE NORMANS established significant bases at Newry, Carlingford, Carrickfergus and Coleraine, all of which soon developed into towns and an infrastructure of estates and monasteries grew up around them. He was married to Affreca, daughter of the king of Man, and she was instrumental in the founding of the Cistercian Grey Abbey in County Down and other monasteries. De Courcy came into conflict with King John, son of Henry II, but defeated his forces in 1204. Finally captured and sent to the Tower of London, he was released after some time and died in France.

One of Ulster's most evocative medieval ruins, Dundrum Castle, was founded by the legendary de Courcy following his invasion of Ulster in 1177. The site occupies the summit of a rocky hill, commanding fine views over Dundrum Bay and the plains of Lecale, controlling access into east

King John ▶

Down from the south. De Courcy's original castle may have had defences of earth and timber, but it is probable that the stone curtain wall of the upper ward was built as early as the 1180s.

As with other early *enceinte* (enclosure) walls, there were no towers, but defence was evidently aided by covered walks with machicolations along the outside wall-head. An early timber hall may have been sited near the keep, where there is a double-latrine in the curtain wall.

▲ *Dundrum Castle, County Down*

The Influence of the Normans

The Norman conquest of Ireland, although impressive, was not systematic and it was to remain incomplete. By the year 1300 it had lost much of its momentum, as events in England and France – as well as several significant military defeats in Ireland itself – drained away much of the manpower and energy needed to sustain the campaign.

NSTEAD, THOSE AREAS controlled by the Normans continued to develop their infrastructures, their towns, their markets and their trading links at home and abroad. At the same time a slow process of assimilation between the two populations was taking place. The descendants of the most powerful Anglo–Norman settlers in Ireland gradually became identified with the native Irish, whose language, habits and laws they adopted to an increasing extent.

The towns remained primarily Norman in population and character. In the rural areas, however, a feudal system of land tenure was established, similar to that found in other parts of western Europe, and many of the Irish continued to live and work on their traditional lands side by side with the Normans. The Norman legal

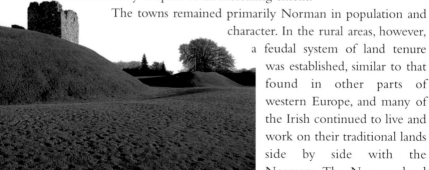

▲ *Norman architecture can be seen throughout Ireland*

▲ *Christ Church Cathedral, Dublin, begun in 1172*

system was introduced into such parts of the island as were reduced to obedience to England.

The church benefited from the coming of the Normans through the introduction of new monastic orders, particularly the Franciscans and the Dominicans. Many of Ireland's most impressive stone-built churches and cathedrals date from this period, and while they are modest in comparison to the great cathedrals of continental Europe, buildings such as St Mary's in Limerick, St Patrick's in Dublin and St Canice's in Kilkenny are an important part of Ireland's Norman heritage. The tomb of Richard de Clare, Strongbow, can still be seen in Christchurch Cathedral in Dublin.

The Defeat of the O'Connors

Despite the fact that the O'Connor kings had acted in good faith as agents of Henry and his successors, it was only a matter of time before the Normans marched on their lands in Connacht.

I N 1235, THEY CROSSED the river Shannon and, sweeping aside any opposition, took what are now the counties of Galway and Mayo. Towns such as Galway, Ballinrobe, Loughrea and Athenry were developed at this time.

Confined to a shrinking kingdom in Connacht, the claim of the O'Connors to be recognised as Ireland's premier royal family became less and less realistic. Following the deaths of Rory in 1198 and of his brother Cathal in

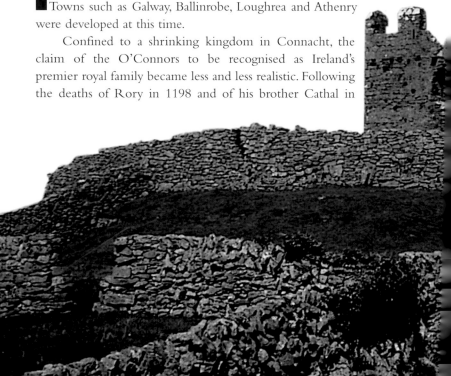

1224, the idea of a Gaelic kingship for the whole of Ireland seemed to have had its day.

However, in 1258, at Caoluisce near Belleek, the sons of the O'Connor king of Connacht and the O'Brien king of Thomond (the family of Brian Boru) acknowledged Brian O'Neill as king of Ireland. This was a short-lived alliance, but it was a sign that the Irish strategy for dealing with the Normans was changing.

Similarly, when, in 1262, several Irish chieftains invited King Haakon of Norway to become their leader in an attack on the Normans, they were for the first time looking to other powers in Europe to help them in their time of trouble. Although this invitation was not accepted it had established a precedent. About the same time, the Irish began to employ the services of Scottish mercenaries, the gallowglass, or *gall-oglaigh* (foreign warriors).

▼ *O'Brien's Castle, County Galway; destroyed by Cromwell in 1652*

Edward Bruce

In 1315, Edward Bruce, brother of Scottish king Robert, landed at Larne, County Antrim, with a Scottish army. He declared himself King of Ireland after taking Carrickfergus. For three years, he did considerable damage to the interests of the colonists in the north-east until he was killed at Faughart, County Louth in October 1318.

ENCOURAGED BY HIS successes, the Irish in Connacht rose, only to be heavily defeated in the bloody Battle of Athenry which claimed the lives of many Connacht chieftains, members of the O'Connor family, and five regional Irish kings.

THE BLACK DEATH

THE BLACK DEATH of 1348–49 also took a terrible toll on the Irish and Normans alike, especially in the towns. So depleted was the Irish economy that Ireland as a colony ceased to be seen as a benefit to England. The immediate impact of the Black Death was general paralysis, as trade ceased and the survivors were in a state of shock.

In an attempt to revive the fortunes of the colony, a series of major campaigns were launched by the English from 1361, culminating in the arrival of Richard II himself in 1394 with a force of nearly 10,000 men. Instability in England itself, though, meant that these expeditions were sporadic rather than sustained.

While these soldiers secured territory and assisted in the enforcement of English law within the colony, there was nothing they could do to help the economic situation. It became clear that Ireland would continue to be a drain on resources rather than an asset.

The plague returned periodically, striking mostly children, until it disappeared from Europe in 1399, not to return again until the seventeenth century. The Black Death changed the demography of Europe substantially. Besides the plague deaths, there was also a decline in birth rate. The net result was that, by 1400, Europe's population was half what it had been in 1345. This is known with some accuracy from many medieval church, census and tax records that have survived. Europe's population took about six generations to recover.

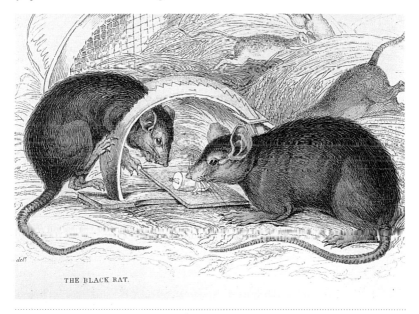

THE BLACK RAT.

▲ Black rats, carriers of the Black Death

The Statutes of Kilkenny

The Norman rulers were alarmed by a situation that saw their people becoming immersed in Irish ways and society. Their influence was dwindling and they attempted to halt this Gaelicisation by introducing the Statutes of Kilkenny in 1366.

THE STATUTES WERE a series of laws enacted by Parliament, meeting in Kilkenny, and aimed primarily at the Normans in the hope of checking assimilation. The wearing of Irish dress, the use of the Brehon Laws and the speaking of the Irish language were all banned. Various other measures were included with the intention of keeping the two peoples apart.

However, despite measures both cultural and military, the Gaelic resurgence continued and the English crown, faced with the cost of a military campaign in Scotland and the Hundred Years War (1338–1453) against France, decided that Ireland for the greater part would have to fend for itself.

▲ *A battle during the Hundred Years' War*

▲ *Ships taking provisions to English troops during Richard II's campaign*

This statute remained inoperative; and although Richard II, king of England, made expeditions into Ireland with large forces later in the fourteenth century, he failed to achieve any practical result. The power and influence of the natives increased so much at the time of the Wars of the Roses that the authority of the English Crown became limited to the area known as the English Pale, a small coastal district around Dublin and the port of Drogheda. Throughout the Wars of the Roses, Ireland supported the ultimate loser – the House of York.

Elsewhere, the English and Normans came together through the necessity of living side by side and also through marriage. Many of the rank and file Normans, and their French colleagues, had little option but to mix in with their English neighbours, leaving their noble masters to carry on the illusion of being truly French.

The Gaelic Recovery

A steady Gaelic revival continued throughout the fourteenth century, with the main skirmishing between the Normans and the Irish taking place on the borders of their respective territories. Gradually, the Normans were pushed back and their influence diluted.

GAELIC IRELAND, with its centuries–old traditions and vigorous language, was revitalising itself. Its customs were revived and many of the most important surviving Gaelic manuscripts, such as the *Leabhar*

Breac and the *Yellow Book of Lecan*, were written in this period. Many of the settlers had married into Gaelic families and, for many of them, Irish became their first language.

Among the various classes of people who devoted themselves to literature in ancient Ireland, there were special annalists, who made it their business to record, with the utmost accuracy, all remarkable events, simply and briefly, without any ornament of language, without exaggeration, and without fictitious embellishment.

▲ *Ireland's traditional language now co-exists with English*

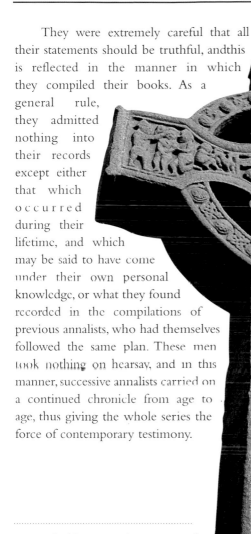

They were extremely careful that all their statements should be truthful, andthis is reflected in the manner in which they compiled their books. As a general rule, they admitted nothing into their records except either that which o c c u r r e d during their lifetime, and which may be said to have come under their own personal knowledge, or what they found recorded in the compilations of previous annalists, who had themselves followed the same plan. These men took nothing on hearsay, and in this manner, successive annalists carried on a continued chronicle from age to age, thus giving the whole series the force of contemporary testimony.

A celtic cross – an important part of Ireland's cultural history ▶

Richard II

The visit of Richard II came about in 1394, when a temporary cessation of hostilities elsewhere presented him with an excellent opportunity to make his presence felt in Ireland.

RICHARD II WON widespread support among the estates in 1395 and 1396 after military successes in Ireland; but as early as 1397 his popular consensus began to unravel. Several events would contribute to Richard's deposition in 1399. These included his marriage to Isabella, princess of France, who was just seven years old; his reluctance to resume the war with France; the impeachments of Thomas Beauchamp, Earl of Warwick, Thomas Arundel, Archbishop of Canterbury, and Thomas of Woodstock, Duke of Gloucester; and his likely complicity in the death of Gloucester at Calais in 1397.

With his mighty army in Ireland, Richard repulsed Art MacMurrough in Leinster and forced the other major Gaelic leaders to submit publicly to him. Thinking that the crisis

◄ *Richard II with his patron saints*

had now been averted, he sailed back to England. Almost immediately, however, fighting broke out again; the king's own heir, Roger Mortimer, was one of those to fall in battle. Fired with anger, Richard returned in 1399 – this was to prove fatal. MacMurrough had learned from his earlier defeat, and proved to be a much more difficult opponent than he had been in Leinster.

Meanwhile, Henry of Lancaster seized the English throne and Richard had to rush back home without completing his business in Ireland. He was forced to abdicate by Henry and died, in 1400, in prison. England's new rulers had enough problems of their own, and Ireland once more was left to its own devices.

Gradually, the Gaelic and the Anglo-Norman elements settled down together and the once-mighty colony shrank to the areas around Dublin on the east coast known as the Pale. Later, historians refer to the Normans becoming 'more Irish than the Irish themselves'.

Art MacMurrough, King of Leinster, in battle ▶

The Wars of the Roses

'Wars of the Roses' is a name given later to a series of battles fought by two rival branches of the Plantagenet dynasty for control of the English throne in the fifteenth century. Each family had a rose as its emblem – white for the York family, red for the House of Lancaster.

▲ *Choosing between the red rose of Lancaster and the white rose of York*

THE FINAL BLOWS in the Wars of the Roses were struck at the Battle of Bosworth Field; the Plantagenet dynasty and the house of York fell with Richard III. It was the last time a king of England led fully armoured medieval knights into battle. The fortunes of Ireland and England became inextricably bound together during this time. Not only had affairs in Ireland contributed to the downfall of Richard II, but the Irish and the Anglo-Irish also had their roles to play in the Wars of the Roses between the Lancastrians and the Yorkists.

In 1449, Richard, Duke of York, was appointed lieutenant, or governor, of Ireland and he made a great impression on the Irish and the Anglo-Irish alike. It became clear that while England still supported Henry VI, Ireland was behind the challenger, Richard of York. This civil war between the noble houses of Lancaster and York had been ongoing since the death of Richard II in 1399. It was Richard's son, Edward IV, who finally triumphed over the House of Lancaster. He ascended to the throne in March 1461, something which brought Ireland and England closer once more.

However, the Wars of the Roses ultimately came to an end with the death of yet another Richard, Richard III (the brother of Edward IV), at the battle of Bosworth Field on 22 August 1485. Richard was killed by followers of the Lancastrian pretender, Henry Tudor.

Richard subsequently went down in history as the last English monarch to die on the battlefield.

▲ *Edward IV, who triumphed over the House of Lancaster*

The Earls of Kildare

This succession of Edward IV also had repercussions for Irish politics. Sir John Butler of Ormond, a supporter of the Lancasters, still hoping to advance their campaign, was defeated in the Roses' bloody battle at Pilltown, near Carrick-on-Suir, by Thomas Fitzgerald, son of the Earl of Desmond. He then succeeded his father as 8th Earl in 1463 and Edward IV, recognising him as the most powerful of the Irish lords, appointed him chief governor of the country.

THE EARL OF Desmond's rule lasted only four years, however, because his close connections with many of the Gaelic chieftains led to suspicions about his loyalty. He was replaced by Sir John Tiptoft, Earl of Worcester, in 1467, tried on a charge of treason and beheaded in Drogheda in February 1468. This action provoked an uprising by both the Gaelic and the Anglo–Irish chiefs, and the Earl of Kildare, who had been similarly accused, was now restored to favour as part of the peace settlement.

▲ *Defeat of the Lancastrians during the Wars of the Roses*

Tiptoft returned to England having failed to enforce English rule despite his many ruthless actions which had earned him the nickname of 'butcher'. He was executed in London when the Lancastrians briefly returned to power in 1470.

Having failed to enforce their rule and without the resources for a full-scale invasion, the English realised they had little alternative but to entrust the running of the country to the major Anglo-Irish lords. With the demise of the Earls of Desmond and Thomond, Garret Mor Fitzgerald, Earl of Kildare, was ideally placed to assume the role of chief governor, which he did in 1478.

▼ *Edward IV*

The Pretenders: Lambert Simnel and Perkin Warbeck

Another advantage Fitzgerald had was that his six daughters were married into several of the most important Anglo-Irish and Gaelic families of the period, including the O'Neills of Tyrone.

DESPITE THIS strong power base, the Earl sought to promote the Yorkist cause rather than establish himself as the potential leader of an independent kingdom in Ireland. So when, in 1487, Lambert Simnel, the Yorkist pretender, arrived in Ireland, he was crowned as Edward VI of England, with the backing of many of the Irish lords. It was the Earl's brother who accompanied him and his army when he returned to England to an ignominious defeat at Stoke.

A second pretender, Perkin Warbeck, arrived in Cork in

HENRY fentencing LAMBERT SIMNEL and his TUTOR

▲ *Henry VII presides over the trial of Lambert Simnel and his tutor*

1491 and both the Earls of Desmond and of Kildare were involved in the plot to make him king of England.

Simnel and Warbeck are early examples of pseudo-princes. They challenged the power of Henry VII of England. Simnel's (c. 1475–1535) birth as the son of a joiner rendered him singularly unqualified to act the role of a great noble and it seems few who had any contact with him were long convinced by the claims made on his behalf.

Warbeck (c. 1474–99), was no greater threat and, like Simnel, was the pawn of others. Of Flemish origin, the son of a minor official, he was persuaded to impersonate Richard, Duke of York, the younger of the two princes murdered in the Tower of London.

The city of Waterford was a host to many royal visits. In 1497, King Henry VII gave the city the name *Urbs Intacta* ('unconquered city') when it refused to recognise Lambert Simnel as king in 1487 and again in 1497 when the pretender Perkin Warbeck was refused recognition.

▲ *Portrait of Henry VII*

Poynings' Law

To counter the threat in Ireland, Henry VII sent a new viceroy, Sir Edward Poynings, a successful soldier and administrator. He summoned the Irish parliament to Drogheda at the end of 1494.

POYNINGS' LAW, as the resultant legislation has been called, aimed to reduce the whole country to obedience and remove for good the threat of Ireland being used as a base by Yorkist pretenders or anyone else who might pose a threat to Henry's crown. The parliament could not be summoned without the knowledge and agreement of the king. All its proposed laws had to be submitted to him for approval as well.

The Irish parliament was made subservient to the British one so that an Irish governor could no longer act independently in a manner that could be construed as being a potential threat to the English king. The Earl of Kildare, Garret Mor Fitzgerald, for instance, had instructed parliament to recognise Lambert Simnel's claim to the throne in 1487. Under Poynings' Law he was now arrested on suspicion of treasonable alliances with the Gaelic chieftains of the north.

The arrest of Kildare provoked yet another uprising and Henry was forced to restore him to power in 1496. 'Since all Ireland cannot rule this man, he shall rule all Ireland,' was the king's opinion. Kildare remained the most important and powerful figure in the country until his death in 1513, when he was succeeded by his son, Garret Og Fitzgerald, as chief governor and Earl of Kildare.

▲ *The Tower of London in the time of Henry VII*

Henry VIII

Born on 28 June 1491, the second son of the Tudor king Henry VII, Henry VIII became heir to the throne when his older brother, Arthur, died in 1502. Henry believed himself to be, without question, the king of God's choice and his rise to the throne, on 21 April 1509, finally affirmed the union of the houses of Lancaster and York

T WAS DURING Henry VIII's reign that religion became, for the first time, a major cause of strife and division in Ireland. The Normans and the Gaels had both professed the same faith though the organisation of the Church differed in areas controlled by the Normans from those areas controlled by the Gaels.

In 1521, Henry had demanded the allegiance of Ireland and had sent the Earl of Surrey to assess the situation. He informed the king that a force of at least 6,000 troops with material support from England would be required. They would have to build castles and other defences in each area

▼ *Marcus Stone's* Henry VIII and Anne Boleyn observed by Queen Catherine

they conquered and follow this up with a colonisation of English people. Past experience had shown that a military presence alone was not sufficient to maintain control of territory.

At the same time, the English Cardinal Wolsey recommended that the Irish Church come under the control of the English Church and be anglicised so that it would not stand in the way of English plans. Neither one of these recommendations was acted on at the time, since Henry considered them both too expensive.

By 1533, however, Henry had married Anne Boleyn and rejected the authority of the Pope, who had refused to allow him a divorce. As a result, the Roman Catholic Church was no longer acceptable in England. From this time on, Henry regarded loyalty to Rome as disloyalty to his own authority.

▲ *Cardinal Wolsey*

Silken Thomas

In 1534, Garret Og, Lord of Kildare, was summoned to England. He left his eldest son, Thomas, Lord Offaly, in charge of his administration. Henry was finally able to break Garret Og's power and incarcerated him in the Tower of London.

THE YOUNG LORD became known as Silken Thomas because of the silken fringes he and his followers wore on their jackets when they rode into Dublin. Striding into the council chamber, he flung down the sword of state, symbol of the king's authority, and declared himself opponent rather than agent of the king.

He rose up against Henry as a result, but Red Piers, seeing the possibility of a final Butler victory over the Geraldine house of Kildare, raised all of Kilkenny and Tipperary against Silken Thomas, who was forced to surrender the following year; he was executed in 1537. The rebellion was ruthlessly put down by the newly appointed deputy, Sir William Skeffington who, with an army of 2,300, overran the Fitzgerald castle at Maynooth, County Kildare, using artillery for the first time in Ireland with great effect.

When the garrison surrendered they were all executed, with the exception of Silken Thomas' infant half-brother. These deeds struck terror into the hearts of the Anglo-Irish lords who had given Silken Thomas at least tacit support for his actions. They too had wished to maintain some independence from the crown and to be able to govern their own affairs. Now, however, when parliament reconvened, keen to show its loyalty to the king, it quickly passed laws similar to those already passed in England, which made Henry VIII head of a state Church.

▼ *Henry VIII*

The Defeat of the House of Kildare

Red Piers Butler, in an attempt to reconcile the Butlers and the Geraldines of Kildare, had married Garret Mor's daughter, Margaret (who became a very famous and much-loved lady in her own right).

HE HAD SLAIN his rival, Sir James Butler, near Kilkenny city in 1497, thereby becoming the agent of the 7th Earl and the most important member of the family in Ireland. If one Irishman could be said to have been responsible for defeat of the House of Kildare it was Red Piers.

With the destruction of the House of Kildare, the balance of power among the Gaelic and Anglo-Irish lords of the midlands was completely changed. Various families and leaders vied for power, but none were to gain the dominant position which the Fitzgeralds had held. Henceforth, the viceroy was always an Englishman and England maintained a permanent garrison in the country.

In 1541, Henry VIII was declared king of Ireland by the subservient

▲ *Traditional fishing methods, still used today, date back to before the Norman invasions*

Irish parliament. He was the first person to be so declared since Edward Bruce. Wishing to bring the whole of the country under his control, he decided that complete Anglicisation was necessary. Where previous administrators had endeavoured to emphasise the differences between the Gaels and the Anglo-Irish and thus keep them segregated, Henry was intent on dealing with them all in a similar fashion.

By insisting on a uniformity of English language, customs and dress throughout the whole kingdom, he was mounting the first serious challenge to the Gaelic culture in many parts of the country. This culture had remained relatively unchanged for several centuries despite the Norman invasions and previous laws enacted against the Irish language and the traditions of Gaelic Ireland.

▲ *Ireland's own language has remained an important part of life*

The Movement Against the Catholic Church

When Henry VIII sought to nullify his first marriage to Catherine of Aragon because of the lack of a male heir, it was clear that Rome would not support him. As a result, in 1531, Henry broke with the Catholic Church and set up a (Protestant) National Church in England under his supreme leadership.

THE DISSOLUTION OF the monasteries from 1536 to 1540, because the crown and the gentry wanted more lands, provoked the northern rising of 1536 to 1537, known as the Pilgrimage of Grace.

As well as the military and legislative onslaught he launched against Gaelic Ireland, Henry also attacked the Church. Because he could brook no opposition and had already broken up the English monasteries following his divorce and disagreements with the Pope, he now wished to promote the

▲ *Anne Boleyn, for whom Henry VIII divorced Catherine of Aragon*

Reformation in Ireland as well. This policy had only limited success, for although he was able to attack the institutions of the Catholic Church, this alone did not guarantee converts to Protestantism. Attempts by his successor Edward VI to introduce doctrinal changes by legislation, after 1547, were resisted and were clearly not sufficient to make people exchange the faith they had professed and practised for 1,000 years. Protestantism was associated with a repressive and unpopular English administration.

English interference under Henry took its toll on the Irish people. In an effort to subdue and rule Ireland, Henry sent Protestants to colonise Ireland and take control from the Gaelic Catholic native population. Subsequent rulers increased the efforts to install plantations, claiming land for England and forcing the Irish to rent their own land back from their conquerors. This effort to 're-colonise' an already thriving civilisation was largely successful, particularly in the area around Dublin in the province of Ulster, and this began the period in Irish history known as the 'Protestant Ascendancy'.

▲ *Edward VI, the son of Henry VIII*

The Death of Shane O'Neill

The strongest opposition to English policies among the chieftains came from Shane O'Neill (*c.* 1530–67), whose father, Conn, had submitted to Henry.

THIS ULSTER CHIEFTAIN now chose to flout the agreement made by Conn, by denying that his father had had the authority to make such an arrangement. He reasserted his family's collective claim to their lands and to their own jurisdiction. For five years, he held off any English advance until he was overthrown and killed by the MacDonnells and Antrim Scots.

▼ *Shane O'Neill, killed by Scottish soldiers*

QUEEN MARY

THE ACCESSION OF MARY, A Catholic, to the English throne brought no relief to the Irish.

Mary I (1516–58), or Mary Tudor, is often referred to as 'Bloody Mary'. She was titled Queen of England and Ireland (1553–58), and of the House of Tudor. The daughter of Henry VIII and Catherine of Aragon, she succeeded to the throne on the death of her half-brother Edward VI and after the deposition of Lady Jane Grey. She married Philip II of Spain (1554), repealed laws establishing Protestantism in England, and re-established Roman Catholicism (1555). She is noted for her persecution of Protestants.

Mary confiscated lands belonging to the O'Moores and the O'Connors in counties Laois and Offaly. She renamed them Queen's and King's County in honour of herself and her husband, and planted them with English settlers.

The dispossessed chieftains waged a guerrilla-type war against the English settlements and became known as Tories, from the Gaelic word for a pursuer (the name is now applied to members of the British Conservative Party). Unable to defeat these Irish, the English summoned the O'Moores and the O'Connors to a conference at Mullaghmast and had them and their families treacherously murdered.

▲ *Mary Tudor*

Queen Elizabeth and Hugh O'Neill

In Ulster, the death of Shane O'Neill (see p.96) left the way open for Hugh O'Neill to succeed him. O'Neill's strong presence in Ulster meant that the English made little progress there.

BY 1570, PRESIDENCIES had been established in Munster and Connacht. These provinces, along with Leinster, were subdivided for administrative purposes into the counties that exist today.

IRELAND
just before
THE ENGLISH INVASION
Scale of English Miles

Munster had been difficult to overcome especially as religion had been a rallying point for the anti-English forces following the ex-communication of Queen Elizabeth I.

Elizabeth I is generally regarded as one of the greatest of English monarchs. As Queen of England, she renewed royal supremacy over the Church. After the defeat of the Spanish Armada in 1588, England became the leading Protestant power and established its basis as a colonial power. The Elizabethan age saw great national vigour, especially in literature.

◀ *A map showing Ireland before the English invasion*

THE BATTLE OF GLENMALURE

THERE WAS AN UPRISING in Munster in 1579 which was assisted by the Spanish and the Italians. This was vigorously put down and the lands belonging to the rebel lords and their families were seized and planted with English colonists. In comparison with Munster, the taking of Connacht was comparatively easy. There was also an uprising in Leinster, led by Viscount Baltinglass and Fiach MacHugh O'Byrne. Their main success was a defeat of the government forces at the Battle of Glenmalure on 25 August 1580.

THE ANGLICISATION OF IRELAND

ON MANY FRONTS, the process of Anglicisation was advancing. Trinity College, Ireland's first university, was opened in 1592, not merely to provide an English education but also to support the established Church. Trinity College is one of Ireland's leading historical sites.

Trinity College, Dublin ▶

Ulster Stands Alone

Only Ulster stood its ground against anglicisation at this time. The chieftains there knew what had happened in the other provinces and had also witnessed the violence and duplicity of the English at first hand.

O N 1575, SORLEY BOY MacDonnell (*Somhairle Buí*) watched helplessly from Torr Head in County Antrim the massacre of the entire population of Rathlin Island. About 600 people died, including his wife and children, whom he had sent there for safety. The massacre was carried out on the orders of the 1st Earl of Essex, who was typical of the military colonists of the time. Not only did they regard the Irish as uncivilised, they also deplored their Catholicism as heresy.

Eager to be successful, they happily got rid of anyone who stood in their way. It was the young Walter Raleigh, for instance, who was in charge at Smerwick in County Kerry in 1580, when some 700 Spaniards and Italians, who had been sent by Philip of Spain and Pope Gregory XIII to help the Irish, were massacred. In return, he was given 4,000 acres of Irish land.

▲ *Sir Walter Raleigh, favourite of Elizabeth I*

Sorley Boy MacDonnell (*c.* 1505–1590) was chief of the MacDonnells of Antrim,. He was at various times in conflict with the English and with neighbouring Gaelic chieftains. He defeated the English at Carrickfergus in 1552, was captured by Shane O'Neill in 1565, only to arrange O'Neill's defeat and death two years later.

After he had lost his family to the English, MacDonnell regained control of the north coast the following year and took his seat at Dunluce Castle. He agreed a truce with the English in 1587. He was succeeded by his son Randal, who was made Earl of Antrim by the English.

▼ *The English colonists viewed Ireland's Catholic faith as heresy*

Hugh O'Neill's Campaign

Hugh O'Neill (*c.* 1550–1616) had been educated in England and so had a better understanding of the English, their mentality, politics and methods than any of his contemporaries.

FOR A NUMBER OF YEARS, he acted ostensibly as part of the English administration, taking their title of Earl of Tyrone in 1585. At the same time, he was building up a series of significant alliances with the major Gaelic families of Ulster.

Through marriage, he brought together the O'Neills and the O'Donnells of Donegal. They had been territorial rivals for many centuries. Elizabeth I was determined to subdue the Gaelic lords of Ulster. To that end, she had the MacMahon chief of Monaghan executed and Red Hugh O'Donnell imprisoned in Dublin Castle.

After the death of Shane O'Neill in 1593, the way was clear for Hugh O'Neill to become the chief of his clan. By 1595, he had dropped all pretence and made it clear where his loyalties really lay. Where previously he had encouraged his supporters to wage

◀ *Queen Elizabeth I*

war on his behalf, he now directly attacked the Blackwater fort and captured it.

The same year he scored a major success over Sir John Norris at Clontibret and, in 1598, with Red Hugh O'Donnell and Hugh Maguire of Fermanagh alongside, he killed Sir Henry Bagenal and heavily defeated his forces at the Battle of the Yellow Ford, near Armagh. O'Donnell, whose escape from Dublin Castle O'Neill had arranged, consolidated Irish predominance in Connacht, while O'Neill himself concentrated on Munster and worked through the midlands.

▲ *Dublin Castle, rebuilt after a fire in 1684*

The Battle of Kinsale

As the rebellion gathered momentum, Elizabeth sent the 2nd Earl of Essex and an army of 20,000 against him. Elizabeth was so annoyed at Essex's lack of success that he was summoned back to London, tried for treason and executed. His successor was Lord Mountjoy, a ruthless strategist with a large army that burned, destroyed and killed everything that crossed its path.

IN 1600, O'NEILL marched north from Munster to assist O'Donnell, who was fighting against an English garrison established at Derry.

In September the same year, the help long promised by Philip of Spain landed at Kinsale, County Cork. However, the Spaniards soon found themselves under siege from Mountjoy and his forces. Encouraged by O'Donnell, O'Neill was forced to march the length of Ireland in the depth of winter to meet the English in an attempt to lift the siege.

A brief and bloody battle ensued at Kinsale on Christmas Eve 1600. It ended in defeat for the Irish. Red Hugh O'Donnell fled Ireland with the Spanish survivors and O'Neill returned to Ulster, his army in tatters. After this, it was only a matter of time before Ulster was taken.

▲ *The army of Queen Elizabeth I marching through Ireland*

The last of the significant Irish chieftains had been defeated; the Spanish attempt at intervention had been thwarted and, with the defeat at the Battle of Kinsale, the old Gaelic order passed into history. Queen Elizabeth herself did not live to witness the surrender of O'Neill at Mellifont in March 1603, but she died knowing that the policies pursued by her and her officials had been successful. Ireland had been taken and beaten into submission.

▲ *Kinsale harbour today*

The Flight of the Earls

Rory O'Donnell, brother of Red Hugh, who had apparently been poisoned by an English agent in Spain in 1602, was now Earl of Tyrconnell and had plotted and planned for revenge without success. He and the new head of the Maguires, Cuchonnacht, had continued to seek Spanish intervention but to no avail.

EVENTUALLY MAGUIRE, regarding the situation as hopeless, chartered a Breton ship to take himself, O'Donnell and 99 other Gaelic chieftains, officials and their families to the Continent. When O'Neill heard of these plans (and having just been officially summoned to London) he decided that he and his family would join the ship. On 4 September 1607, they sailed from Rathmullen, County Donegal, an event now known as the 'Flight of the Earls'. They landed in the Spanish Netherlands and travelled across Europe to Rome, where O'Neill was to live in exile until his death in 1616.

Their departure left the way open for the most radical form of the government's policy of plantation yet. The leaderless Irish were to be confined to the poorest areas, while the counties of Armagh, Cavan, Coleraine, Donegal, Fermanagh and Tyrone were to be divided into lots of 1,000–2,000 acres and given to 'undertakers': people who undertook to manage these new estates, build defences, and settle them with Protestant families who were either English or from the Scottish lowlands.

The territory that lay between the northern rivers, the Foyle and the Bann, Coleraine, County Derry, had its own particular arrangement, being given to the City of London. The City undertook to rebuild Derry, and, with the addition of a piece of Tyrone, became the county of Londonderry, a particular element of the anglicisation process that still causes disagreement to this day.

▲ *An image of Londonderry, c. 1680*

The Plantation of Ulster

From 1603 to 1607, Ulster remained in a state of unease while its future was decided. Lord Mountjoy, O'Neill's adversary, had become a supporter of the settlement agreed between the government and the chieftains.

HIS DEATH IN 1606, however, led to the arrival of Chichester as Lord Deputy and of Sir John Davies, who were both eager to see the anglicisation of Ulster, particularly Davies, who foresaw rich pickings there for the crown.

Although the government forces now controlled the greater part of the land, their efforts to impose Protestantism as the state religion met with little success in the majority of the country. The only amenable area was the heavily planted counties of Ulster. Most of the new planter families were Protestant in name at least, but the vast majority of the Irish people remained steadfastly Catholic.

▲ *Ulster was in a state of unrest for the first years of the 17th century*

Under the Plantation of Ulster, in 1610, grants were made to five Scottish settlers in the barony of Tullyhunco. The first of these, consisting of 2,000 acres, was granted to Sir Alexander Hamilton of Endervicke, in Scotland. The lands were to be created into the manor of Clonkine and Carrotubber, with 600 acres in demesne. He was also granted the advowson and patronage of the rectory of Killeshandra.

His son, Sir Claud, was granted 1,000 acres near the Leitrim border. It was to be created into the manor of Clonyn or Taghleagh. Two brothers, Alexander and John Achmootie (or Auchmothy) each received 1,000 acres, to be created into the manors of Kilegh and Dromheada, respectively. This process was repeated throughout the county, to the great dismay of the Catholic native population.

Lord Mountjoy, who was created Earl of Devonshire in 1603 ▶

The Counter-Reformation

The Counter-Reformation is the name given to the movement in the sixteenth and seventeenth centuries that arose as a reaction to the Protestant Reformation.

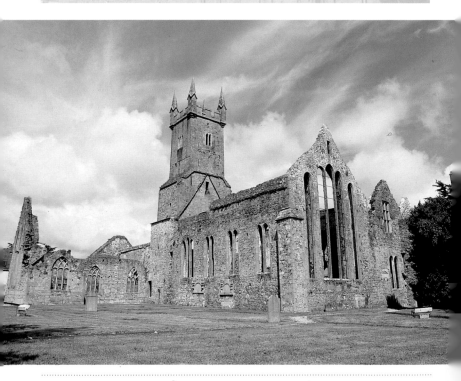

▲ *A ruined Franciscan church*

U NTIL RECENTLY, HISTORIANS have tended to stress the negative and repressive elements in this movement, such as the 'Inquisition' and the 'Index of Forbidden Books', and to concentrate their attention on its political, military and diplomatic aspects. They now show greater appreciation for the high level of spirituality that animated many of the leaders of the Counter-Reformation.

Religion became the most important element that united the Gaelic Irish and the old Anglo-Irish aristocracy. England, with its Protestant monarchy, was in conflict with the Spanish and the French.

This was now the period of the Counter-Reformation. While the Catholic faith was under severe military, legal and economic pressure in Ireland, a network was soon established between the exiled Gaelic chieftains, the Irish monasteries and seminaries on the Continent, and the various international religious orders that aimed to counter the advance of Protestantism in Ireland.

Sons of the various chieftains who left Ireland in 1607 either joined various continental armies or studied for the priesthood in colleges as far away as Prague and Salamanca. The Church, which from its arrival in Ireland had sought to record the traditions and language of Ireland, continued to do so. The history of the country was seen as an important part of the work of the Counter-Reformation.

To understand history from the point of view of the native Irish, it is necessary to study the *Annals*. These list events in Ireland from the earliest times in chronological order, and include such diverse matter as battles, marriages, successions of kings, murders, comets, storms and deaths of abbots and poets. Of all the surviving *Annals*, the *Annals of the Four Masters* are the most important.

The 1641 Rebellion

The years directly preceding the outbreak of the Rebellion and the political climate of both England and Ireland at the time offer an important insight into the inevitable course the Irish state took at the time of the uprising.

THE REBELLION TOOK PLACE at a time of sweeping turmoil throughout the British Isles, as Charles I attempted to maintain control over Ireland and his own parliament.

The year 1641, then, saw another major rising in Ireland. The native people of Ulster, who had never accepted the violence and injustice of the Plantation of their lands, now saw England's difficulty as Ireland's opportunity. They were also afraid that if either the Scots or the English parliament became more powerful than the king, conditions for them would deteriorate rapidly.

◀ *King Charles I*

This was because both the Scots and the English parliaments were aggressively Protestant in thought, word and deed.

On the eve of a planned attack on Dublin Castle, the seat of English authority in Ireland, however, the rising was compromised, its leaders were arrested and the attack never took place. In Ulster, however, the rising went ahead and initially met with considerable success under Sir Phelim O'Neill.

The 1641 Rebellion, and the ensuing occupation of Ireland by Oliver Cromwell, would prove to have lasting effects on the modern Irish state. There were several distinct factors that ultimately led to the advent of the 1641 uprising, representing the independent interests of different factions within Ireland. The two most prominent were the almost complete disenfranchisement of the native Irish Catholics and the increasing seizure of land and power from the established English settlers, also known as the 'Old English'.

▲ *Oliver Cromwell*

The Confederation of Kilkenny

In 1642, the outbreak of hostilities in England between Charles I and his parliament led to shortages for parliament's forces in Ireland.

THEY WERE COMPELLED to garrison themselves in towns like Trim and Drogheda, and embarked on campaigns to seize supplies for themselves, while at the same time destroying crops and livestock to prevent the enemy getting their hands on them.

After securing Ulster, Sir Phelim O'Neill marched on Drogheda, where he was joined by the Old English and Anglo-Irish, who feared the growing power of the English parliament. Others joined the rising across the country and the English government, realising that the situation was very serious, borrowed heavily to finance a major operation.

The Irish, better organised than before, met in Kilkenny in October 1642 to consolidate their gains. This Confederation of Kilkenny effectively became Ireland's new government and news of its success brought Irishmen who had extensive military experience in continental armies back from exile to continue the struggle. The most significant of these was Owen Roe O'Neill.

▲ *Charles I with members of his Parliament*

THE BATTLE OF BENBURB

OWEN ROE O'NEILL (Eoghan Rua O'Neill) (c. 1584–1649) was born in County Armagh and was a nephew of Hugh O'Neill. He had been educated at Louvain and had served in the Spanish army in Flanders for nearly 40 years. He returned to Ireland in 1642 and took control of the Irish forces in Ulster.

He was a superb military strategist and scored an impressive victory over a Scottish army at Benburb in County Tyrone in 1646. It was rumoured at his death in 1649, that he may have been poisoned. He typified the spirit of Irish Catholicism that was nurtured by the Counter-Reformation movement among Irish exiles on the Continent.

▼ *County Tyrone, where O'Neill won victory over the Scots*

The English Civil War

In March 1642, Charles, believing that parliament had gone too far when it issued the Grand Remonstrance, moved to arrest John Pym and four other leaders. Charles himself entered parliament with solders and a warrant, but Pym and the others were gone, having been tipped off in advance.

THEY FLED TO LONDON where they were hidden by Puritan loyalists, who dominated the city government. The king demanded the return of Pym, but the citizens refused. London, at least, was in rebellion.

That summer parliament, fearing military action, tried to seize control of the army by issuing orders for soldiers to report to parliamentary, rather than royal, representatives. The king countered by ordering that the bill be ignored and raised

▲ *The Houses of Parliament in London, dominated by Puritan loyalists in the 1600s*

his own army in August. Some turned out for the King, some for Parliament, and the war was on.

Those loyal to parliament were called Roundheads; those loyal to the king were Cavaliers. The Independents dominated the parliamentary army. Royalist strength lay in the north and west; Roundhead strength was in the south and especially in London. Parliament was now free of the king and it passed numerous reforms.

Events in England had complicated the situation greatly. Charles was now in open conflict with the English parliament and O'Neill's victory over the Scottish was seen as a victory for the king. Charles had an army in Ireland, which he would rather have used against his own parliament in the on-going English Civil War, and the parliamentarians, too, would rather have directed their resources away from Ireland at this time.

The Irish sought to wrest concessions and promises from Charles, unaware that the greatest threat came from the growing strength of the parliamentarians. Nothing decisive was to happen in Ireland until 1649, when Charles was defeated, tried and executed.

The execution of Charles I ▶

Oliver Cromwell

Once the parliamentarians had gained full control of power in England, they moved swiftly against the Irish.

FULL OF FEAR and loathing of Catholicism and angered by exaggerated reports of Irish atrocities against the Ulster planters in 1641, the Puritan army of the new Lord Lieutenant, Oliver Cromwell, landed in Dublin in August 1649. They were intent on revenge and the eradication of the Irish problem once and for all.

Cromwell's 20,000-strong army crushed all military opposition. Bishop Heber MacMahon of Clogher, who had become leader of Owen Roe O'Neill's army after his death in 1649, was captured and executed in Enniskillen, where his head was placed on a spike at the castle.

The royalist forces under Sir Arthur Aston, an English Catholic, had their headquarters in the heavily fortified town of Drogheda, which they believed they could defend. However, Cromwell's artillery breached the walls and the town was captured on 11 September. Cromwell ordered that all the soldiers of the garrison should be executed. In the orgy of killing that followed, over

◄ *A portrait of Oliver Cromwell in 1647*

3,500 people, including women and children, were slaughtered. When the garrison of Wexford suffered a similar fate, other towns chose to surrender rather than be destroyed.

The second target for Cromwell's wrath was the Catholic Church, whose property was seized and destroyed and whose priests were hunted down. Thus much of the man-power and organisation which had been built up as part of the Counter-Reformation movement were lost. By May 1650, Cromwell was able to return to England, confident that his work in Ireland was done.

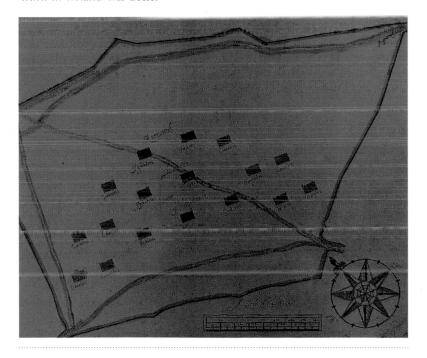

▲ *Plan of Cromwell's army encampment near Dublin, 1649*

The Fallout from Cromwell's Campaign

The retribution for the rebellion was swift and severe. Catholic landowners who had been implicated in the rising lost all their lands and property. Others were allowed to retain a portion, but not of the same lands.

INSTEAD THESE MEN were transplanted to Connacht and to Clare, west of the river Shannon, where they could be kept under close scrutiny. From this time comes the dreaded phrase 'to Hell or to Connacht', which means having no choice at all.

Many women and children, defeated soldiers and priests were shipped off to the West Indies to be sold as slaves. These were to be the ancestors of the so-called 'Black Irish' of Monserrat, the Caribbean island where Irish was still spoken up to 100 years ago by a mixed-race people.

▲ *Fighting between Catholics and Protestants*

All the confiscated land was to be used to pay for the war, with blocks of land being allocated to officers and men for their services. Many sold their holdings and returned to England. As a result, the influx of Protestants was not as great as it might have been. Nevertheless, the Cromwellian policies resulted in a major change in the ownership of land.

In those 26 counties, excluding Connacht and Clare, land ownership was exclusively in Protestant hands. The effect was not the same as that created by the Plantation of Ulster, where many of those who now lived and worked off the land and who peopled the towns were Protestant. Instead, this policy replaced all the major Catholic landowners with Protestants and created a new land-owning upper class, not a community with a significant Protestant population.

The restoration of the monarchy under Charles II in 1660 brought little change. Those Catholics in Ireland who had supported the royalist cause were to be disappointed if they thought the king would reward their loyalty by restoring their lands.

Charles II, who ignored the Irish cause ▶

St Oliver Plunkett

On 30 September 1629 Oliver Plunkett was born at his family home at Loughenew, in the county of Meath. He was the last Catholic to die for his faith at Tyburn.

OLIVER PLUNKETT WAS educated by the Jesuits at the then newly established Irish College. He was ordained in 1654 and appointed Archbishop of Armagh and Primate of all Ireland by Pope Clement IX.

In 1679, Plunkett was arrested and put on trial at Dundalk, for conspiring against the state by plotting to bring 20,000 French soldiers into the country and levelling a tax on his clergy to support 70,000 men for rebellion. Lord Shaftesbury, under King Charles II, knew that the Archbishop would never be convicted in Ireland, he was therefore removed to Newgate prison in London.

In June 1681, Archbishop Plunkett was found guilty by the jury of high treason, and the Primate of All Ireland was condemned to be hanged, disembowelled. and quartered. He was executed on 1 July 1681. There were several priests present at the gallows, and one of them, Father Gasper, a Belgian Carmelite attached to the Spanish Embassy, pronounced the words of absolution from sin as the still-living body was cut down. The hangman removed the head from the body and threw it into the fire (it was rescued before being incinerated).

Plunkett's body was placed in two tin boxes and buried next to five Jesuits who had been executed before him. It was then moved to the Benedictine monastery in Lambspring Germany and, 200 years later, in 1883, was transported again to Downside Abbey, in England. The martyr's head is preserved in St Peters Church at Drogheda. In 1975, some of the remains were returned to Ireland, when he was canonized.

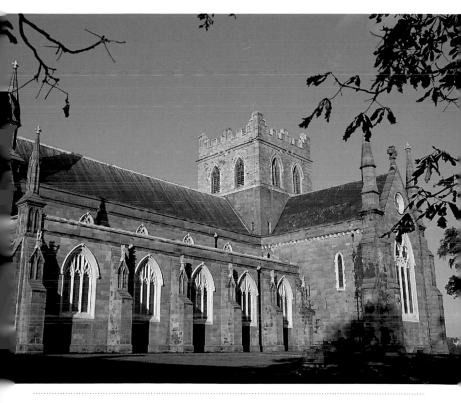

▲ *Armagh Cathedral, of which Oliver Plunkett was Archbishop*

The Siege of Derry

King James II converted to Catholicism after his marriage to Mary, the daughter of the Italian Duke of Modena.

JAMES LEFT ENGLAND in 1679 and did not return until 1685 when he succeeded his brother to the throne. Many Cromwellian settlers, fearing a change of policy, left Ireland at this time. James, however, was in a weak and precarious position and any changes he mooted were of a minor nature.

In 1688, Lord Danby, the leader of the Whigs sent for William of Orange, a Dutch prince who was married to James's protestant daughter Mary. The crisis had been sparked, in 1688, with the birth of James's son. The baby's arrival had caused English establishment to panic that this was the start of a new Catholic dynasty.

▲ *King James II, who converted to Catholicism*

William and Mary were declared joint rulers and James was forced to flee to the Court of Louis XIV in France for help. He then travelled to Ireland expecting to find more supporters among the Catholics there.

James arrived in Kinsale from the court of Louis XIV with a small French army. Louis at the time was at war with the Grand Alliance of Spain, England, Holland, Bavaria, Austria and the Pope. In Ireland, James's deputy was Richard Talbot, Earl of Tyrconnell and brother of the Archbishop of Dublin, Peter Talbot, who had been arrested around the same time as Oliver Plunkett and had died in gaol.

Talbot convened a Catholic parliament and mustered a Catholic army, aiming to secure Ireland for James. In the north, however, most of the English settlers and soldiers were Protestants and they sided with William of Orange. Towns such as Derry and Enniskillen declared their allegiance to him.

Talbot marched on Derry, hoping to dislodge the disloyal garrison, but a number of apprentice boys, who were in the town as part of the development plan organised by the City of London and its guilds, shut the gates, preventing the Jacobite forces from entering. The subsequent siege of Derry, which lasted for 105 days in 1689, was eventually lifted when further English regiments and supply ships relieved the beleaguered town.

William and Mary ▶

The Battle of the Boyne

The Dutch general Schomberg also landed in the north with 15,000 reinforcements. He captured Carrickfergus and marched on Dundalk. Suffering heavy losses, he in turn was forced to seek reinforcements.

THESE WERE HEADED by William himself, who also landed at Carrickfergus with an assortment of regiments, including German, Danish and French Huguenot troops which, when combined with Schomberg's forces, numbered some 35,000 well-armed and well-equipped soldiers.

James's forces, on the other hand, numbered no more than 25,000, including English regiments which were still loyal, French troops sent by Louis XIV and some Irish infantry and cavalry. The two sides met at the River Boyne in County Meath on 1 July 1690, where William was victorious despite the death of Schomberg.

The Battle of The Boyne is the victory now celebrated by Orangemen on 12 July each year. This change in date allows for the change from the Julian to the Gregorian calendar in 1752.

◀ *William III at the Battle of the Boyne, where he defeated James II*

Louis XIV of France, supporter of James II ▶

The Siege of Limerick

James fled back to France while his army regrouped and marched across the country; they suffered further defeats at Athlone and at Aughrim.

T WAS ONLY WHEN William twice laid siege to Limerick, where the Irish were commanded by Patrick Sarsfield (*c.* 1655–93), that William met with serious resistance and was forced to sign a treaty, the Treaty of Limerick, on 3 October 1691.

Under this treaty, religious freedom and the rights of the native Irish were to be restored in return for the disbanding of Sarsfield's army, some 14,000 of whom were also permitted to go to the Continent, where many

▼ *James fleeing from Ireland after the Battle of the Boyne*

joined the armies of France, Spain and other European powers, often forming special Irish brigades or regiments.

Over the ensuing 100 years, up to 500,000 Irish are believed to have fought in foreign armies. These men are known as the 'wild geese'. Under the Penal Laws of the eighteenth century, Irish Catholics were not allowed to join the British Army.

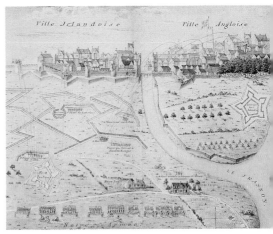

▲ *View of Limerick in c. 1691*

THE PENAL LAWS

THE POLICIES OF THE Irish government sought to strengthen the position of the Protestant ascendancy in Ireland, something that gave England security. This also gave the Protestants the opportunity to make things as favourable as possible for themselves by methods which were not necessary for the preservation of England's interests.

For instance, a Catholic was not allowed to own a horse worth more than five pounds and if he was offered five pounds for his horse, he was legally obliged to sell it. These Penal Laws, such as 'The Act to Prevent the Further Growth of Popery' (1704), forced all those who would not, or could not, conform to the Anglican Church and way of life down onto the bottom rung of society.

As well as being virulently anti-Catholic, these laws also affected the dissenters in the northern counties, although to a lesser extent. All important offices and positions were open only to Protestants. In this way, Catholics were excluded from all political power.

Their ownership of land, which had already dwindled to just a small fraction of what they had once held, was further reduced as landed gentry faced the choice of conforming to Protestantism or seeing their estates broken up by inheritance laws, which stipulated that Catholic estates were to be divided equally between all a landowner's sons. The purchase of land was also forbidden.

Soon Catholics were also prohibited from conducting schools or sending their children abroad to be educated, and from voting in parliamentary elections. Bishops and members of religious orders were banished and ordinary priests had to register their names and parishes and promise to uphold the law.

With no education system, no ordinations (as bishops were required for these) and no new clergy permitted to enter the country from abroad, it was expected that the Roman Catholic clergy would die out within a generation. However, it is clear that many still managed to go abroad to attend the Irish seminaries in continental Europe. It was at these colleges that all Irish Catholic clergy were educated until the founding of Maynooth College in 1795.

▲ *Maynooth College, County Kildare*

THE REFUTATION OF THE TREATY OF LIMERICK

APART FROM ALLOWING Sarsfield and his army to leave Ireland, the Treaty of Limerick was not implemented, and most of the promises made therein were subsequently cancelled by the English parliament. The eighteenth century saw the harshest series of anti-Catholic laws yet drawn up and implemented by the now exclusively Protestant parliament in Dublin with the prior arrangement and agreement of the king and his ministers. English policy sought to ensure that Ireland would not be a threat to its well-being economically, politically nor militarily. Ireland's export trade was destroyed and the country was treated as another colony whose natural resources were there to be exploited.

WESTMINSTER DIRECT RULE

IN 1720, AN ACT WAS PASSED which gave Westminster the right to legislate directly for Ireland, which meant that the Irish parliament could be easily overruled.

▼ *The Houses of Parliament in Westminster*

Protestant Ascendancy

By 1778, only five per cent of Irish land was in Catholic hands, even though Catholics made up 75 per cent of a population which had grown rapidly through the century and was approaching five million by 1800.

FOR THE PROTESTANT aristocracy, however, the eighteenth century was a golden era. Landlords grew rich and built palatial residences on their largest estates, while the tenant farmers struggled to pay their rents and tithes to a church to which very few of them belonged. Dublin developed as a city, boasting fine architecture and broad streets.

For the tenant farmers, it was a time of great hardship. Many of them lived in abject poverty, barely managing to survive from year to year. In years when the crops failed, many died simply because they had absolutely nothing else to fall back on. In 1727–30, a harsh famine devastated south of the country.

By 1740–41, the crisis was country-wide and a large number of people died from hunger and disease. An economic condition dictated by London discouraged tillage in order to protect the English producers; as a result, during the middle decades of the eighteenth century, Ireland was forced to import more grain than she exported.

In 1759, the ban on Irish cattle exports to England was lifted; this had the effect of reducing the amount of tillage land further as more and more was given over to pasture. As this type of farming was less labour-intensive, many people were cleared off the land and left destitute.

▼ *The style of thatched croft lived in by tenant farmers*

◄ *Castletown House, County Kildare, built in the 18th century*

The Decline of Gaelic Ireland

While the Protestant landlords lived a merry, and extravagant, life the 'Flight of the Wild Geese', which had been encouraged by the Treaty of Limerick and by the prevailing social conditions, continued to reduce the status and manpower of the old Gaelic aristocratic families in Ireland.

THE ORDINARY IRISH PEOPLE, despite their near–impossible living conditions, retained a respect for learning and education. By their use of unofficial schools (hedge-schools) and travelling schoolmasters, they maintained their own culture, language and traditions as well as a knowledge of the classics. The poets and harpers, now deprived of the status and patronage they once enjoyed, still had an audience, sometimes in the grand houses of the landlords, but more often among their own people.

Turlough O'Carolan (1670–1738), the most renowned of the harpers, has left many of his songs and compositions, all but one in Irish and many of which are dedicated to his Protestant patrons in the north-west. Gaelic stories and poetry continued to be produced, and since there was no opportunity available for their publication, a new vernacular literature developed which was transmitted orally and circulated in manuscript form. Just as in earlier times, these manuscripts were jealously guarded and carefully copied.

This activity continued in many areas up until the Great Famine of the 1840s, often as part of a culture ignored, despised and ridiculed – or

The Book of Durrow, *which was carefully guarded in uncertain medieval times* ▶

indeed often totally hidden from – the middle and upper classes. Enniskillen, for instance, a planter and garrison town in Ulster, was home to Simon Macken, an important scribe, until his death in 1836.

'Whiteboys' and 'Defenders'

During the eighteenth century, agrarian rebels formed themselves into secret societies. They went by the names of 'Whiteboys', 'Oak Boys', 'Rockites', 'Ribbonmen', 'Defenders' and such like.

GRIEVANCES SUCH AS evictions or ill-treatment of tenants by landlords and agents, and land–grabbing (taking the holding of an evicted tenant) were punished by violent methods. There were killings and house burnings, but more often, revenge was in the form of damage to animals, sending cows over cliffs, cutting off the hooves of cattle, hamstringing horses, clubbing dogs to death, burning stables with the animals inside. In the 1760s, complete villages were cleared in Tipperary. Land that had been held as common land was now enclosed.

The 'Whiteboys' – so-called because they wore white smocks over their clothes as a disguise – began a campaign of violence and intimidation against landlords' agents and those who collected tithes. As many of the landlords were absentees, they did not feel the full effect of this campaign, but it soon spread to other parts of the country. Repressive measures were introduced by the government that made involvement in Whiteboy activities a capital offence. Local magistrates and landlords were very active in the suppression of the movement. Although the illegal activities abated, sporadic actions continued

The cleared village of Tipperary ▶

well into the nineteenth century, because the root cause of the Whiteboys' grievances had never been addressed.

In the northern counties, the 'Hearts of Oak' and the 'Hearts of Steel' also emerged briefly in response to particular local grievances. Growing Catholic confidence and economic strength was seen as a threat and sectarian tensions grew, especially in rural areas of Ulster. The Catholics had a secret organisation called the 'Defenders', the Protestant equivalent was the 'Peep o' Day Boys'.

The Northern Situation

In Ulster, the Protestant tenant farmers had a greater security of tenure than their Catholic counterparts in Ireland as a whole.

THEY ALSO BENEFITED from the growth in the linen industry, and because the army and the professions were open to them, a Protestant middle class developed that could freely engage in commerce and politics.

▲ *Map showing the old provinces of Ireland*

The influence and size of this new class grew as the century progressed. Towns such as Belfast became prosperous, but this prosperity was reserved for non-Catholics. There were only seven Catholics in Belfast in 1708 and, 50 years later, Catholics made up only six per cent of the town's population.

Although the Presbyterian population's position was not as straitened as the Catholics, they nevertheless resented the limitations placed on them and, during the eighteenth century, large numbers of them emigrated to North America, where they played a significant role in the development of what was to become the United States in 1776.

The first recorded sailing of an emigrant ship from Ulster to America was that of the *Friends' Goodwill*, which left Larne in April 1717 for Boston, Massachusetts. The exodus had started.

Five thousand people would leave Ulster that year, looking for a new life in America. Their journeys laid the foundations for future immigration and settlement. The letters that returned to their homeland never attempted to conceal the hardships and hazards of a sea journey that could, in some cases, last up to three months in cramped and unhygienic conditions. However, the message remained that the journey was still worth enduring, as the rewards waiting in America were great.

▼ *Early Irish farming methods are still used today*

The Founding of the Orange Order

Although, in theory, Ireland was now a separate entity with loyalty to the king, this did not automatically mean any major changes in policy.

MANY OF THOSE in parliament were members of the landed aristocracy and were not keen to see any further concessions to the Catholic Irish, feeling that this would threaten their position. Once again, they chose to suspect Catholics of disloyalty and claimed they were likely to ferment revolution in league with England's enemies, especially France.

The relaxation of anti-Catholic legislation, especially that relative to land tenure, created a panic among the entire Protestant population. As a dominant minority, they always felt that their position needed to be guarded and greatly feared the rise of the Catholic underclasses.

The Protestant equivalent to the Catholic 'Defenders' was the 'Peep o' Day Boys'. There were various confrontations and violent incidents between these two groups, the most significant of which was the so-called 'Battle of the Diamond'. This took place at a crossroads near Loughgall, in County Armagh, on 21 September 1795. Here the local Peep o' Day Boys confronted a group of Catholic Defenders and killed 30 of them. That evening the Peep o' Day Boys met again at the house of one of their members, and the first Orange Order Lodge was established. Less than a year later, there were 90 lodges commemorating the anniversary of the Battle of the Boyne on 12 July.

At this meeting, the Peep o'Day Boys resolved 'that at all times they would stand together, fight for the faith of the Reformed Church, and by all lawful means support, maintain and defend the Sovereign and Protestant Succession to the Throne, and to the utmost of their power keep the peace and the public safety'.

◀ *The Irish House of Commons in 1780*　　　　*The Battle of the Boyne* ▲

'Grattan's Parliament'

The second half of the eighteenth century saw two events that made a huge impression on public and political opinion in Ireland.

THE FIRST WAS THE American War of Independence, fought against the British, and the second was the French Revolution, with its slogan of 'Liberty, Equality and Fraternity'.

The British government, sensing that any trouble in Ireland could have serious consequences, moved to reduce restrictions against Catholics. By allowing them to join the army, they hoped to replenish its dwindling ranks.

In the 1770s, moves were made to repeal the Penal Laws. Inheritance and land tenure laws were changed and the constitutional amendments of 1782 removed Westminster's power to legislate directly for Ireland. Poynings' Law of 1495 was also amended. The reformed Irish parliament, which lasted until the Act of Union in 1880, would later be referred to as 'Grattan's Parliament'.

Henry Grattan (1746–1820) was a Dublin-born lawyer, who entered the Irish parliament in 1775. In 1782, when Dublin gained a measure of legislative independence, he proclaimed in parliament 'Ireland is now a nation ... she is no longer a wretched colony'. A colourful figure, Grattan later campaigned against the Act of Union and in favour of Catholic emancipation. He is now seen to have been more popular than he was politically significant. Certainly, there was much celebration in 1782, and parliament voted its hero £50,000 in gratitude.

The final years of the century saw great commercial activity, and a prosperous Dublin acquired many of the handsome Georgian buildings for which it is noted today.

Henry Grattan, pioneer of Irish independence ▶

◀ *The French Revolution*

The United Irishmen

In 1791, an organisation had been formed that hoped to attract people of different religious persuasions and unite them in a campaign for greater economic and political independence from Britain. This was the Society of United Irishmen.

ITS PRIME MOVER was a Kildare-born lawyer, Theobold Wolfe Tone. Tone (1763–98), a political theorist, was strongly influenced by the events and philosophies of the French Revolution. He held the view that Ireland should be a non-sectarian independent republic. He was a supporter of Catholic rights and published a pamphlet, *An Argument of Behalf of the Catholics of Ireland*, in 1791.

In Belfast, he enthusiastically joined the Society of United Irishmen which had been founded there the same year. Coming to Belfast, he found a lively city with a political culture that was much more open than that in Dublin, which was dominated by the aristocracy.

Belfast's businessmen provided him with a much more liberal audience, and they were impressed with what he had to say. His demands

▲ *Theobald Wolfe Tone*

for parliamentary reform pleased them, as many were Presbyterians who felt that a parliament full of major Protestant landowners was not one likely to represent the interests of the mercantile classes.

Returning to Dublin, he established a branch of the organisation there. The movement became increasingly radical, and as the government appeared to be dragging its feet about reform, the United Irishmen began to consider military options. Tone sought help from France, but the agent he dealt with was compromised by an informer. The Dublin branch of the organisation was suppressed and Tone was forced to flee to America to avoid arrest. From America, he went to France where he continued to lobby for a French invasion.

▲ *Wolfe Tone was a staunch supporter of Catholic rights*

Rebellion in the South-East

The government was ready to suppress the new threat. It encouraged the establishment of a militia in 1793 and of the yeoman corps in 1794.

THESE WERE OFTEN under the leadership of the local landlord or magistrate. By forming these forces, the government was able to free many units of regular troops for duties elsewhere.

The yeoman corps were often dominated by Orangemen and were given a free rein in their actions, as their commanders were often also the local magistrates. The heavy-handedness of the government's response to the agitations of the United Irishmen only increased their desire to gain radical reforms, religious freedom and political independence. It also drove the movement underground and made it potentially more dangerous.

More efficient against the United Irishmen than the aggression of the yeomanry, was the government's network of informers. In March 1798, the Leinster directory of the movement were all arrested during a meeting in a Dublin house. Only Lord Edward

▲ *The arrest and wounding of Lord Edward Fitzgerald*

Fitzgerald (1763–98), son of the Duke of Leinster, escaped. However, he was mortally wounded several weeks later, during his arrest after his hiding place had been discovered.

Fitzgerald, the son of the first Duke of Leinster and maternal grandson of the Duke of Richmond, showed an early liking for the military life and joined the Sussex Militia in 1779. He served and was severely injured in America. Returning to Ireland he sat in the Irish parliament for Athy before rejoining the army for an adventurous journey through uncharted parts of Canada. He returned to the Irish parliament as MP for Kildare, but his increasing attraction to the new thinking inspired by the French Revolution led him to visit Paris in 1792.

When it did happen, the rising lacked leadership and its efforts were patchy in the area around Dublin.

▼ *The Government Buildings, Dublin*

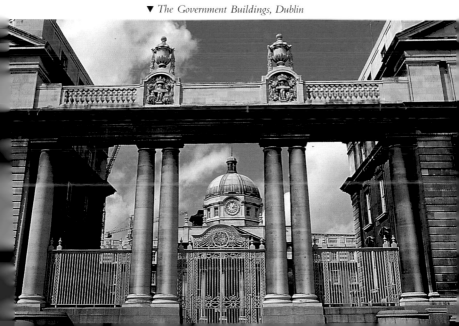

Rebellion in Antrim and Down

In Ulster, the strength of the United Irishmen had already been sapped the previous year by the ruthless actions of General Lake and the yeomanry, whose actions were often motivated by sectarianism. Lake's powers were absolute and the terror and destruction he caused forced many into submission.

THE LEADER OF the rebellion in Ulster was Henry Joy McCracken, but he was soon defeated by Colonel Durham's militia at Antrim and Henry Munro, the leader at Ballinahinch in County Down, held out for only three days before being captured.

▲ *Father Murphy, one of McCracken's fellow rebel leaders*

▲ *Humbert surrenders after the Battle of Ballinamuck*

McCracken (1767–98) was born into a prosperous Presbyterian family with various business interests in Belfast. He was one of the founder members of the United Irishmen in that city. He was arrested in 1796. Although he had been a prominent figure in the founding and organising of the United Irishmen in Belfast and surrounding counties, he was not directly involved in the events of 1798. Nonetheless, he was hanged in Downpatrick for his believed role in the activities.

French involvement in the campaign was of a minor nature as, by this time, Napoleon had turned his attention to Egypt. The small force led by General Humbert did not arrive in Killala until August 1798 – after the main rising had been suppressed. The Irish troops were severely depleted by the suppressed rising, and the French were forced to surrender after the unsuccessful Battle of Ballinamuck in County Longford. They were defeated by the superior forces of the government led by the viceroy, Lord Cornwallis. Humbert is still remembered in many parts of County Mayo, and the French element of Irish history is frequently celebrated.

The Aftermath of the Death of Wolfe Tone

Another small French expedition later sailed for Ireland, but the British navy captured most of the French ships in October 1798 off Lough Swilly, County Donegal. Among the French officers captured was Wolfe Tone, who was recognised and betrayed by an old college friend.

TONE WAS THEN brought to Dublin, where he was found guilty by court martial and condemned to death. He apparently committed suicide in prison before he could be executed.

Another conspirator, William Henry Hamilton, who had also been on board a French ship and who was also to play a significant role in Emmet's rising in 1803, was more fortunate. His ship was escorted to Liverpool, from where he was deported to France, his command of the French language being so good that he successfully passed himself off as a French officer.

William Pitt, the British prime minister, realised that urgent and drastic action was required in Ireland, and that military action alone, no matter how repressive and reactive, would not suffice.

Having earlier considered declaring Great Britain and Ireland a great free-trade area, he now planned to unite the Irish and British parliaments

▲ *The capture of Wolfe Tone*

and in effect to make Ireland a part of the United Kingdom. The proposal was debated in the Irish parliament in 1799. After a number of spirited contributions, led by Henry Grattan, who emphasised Ireland's own separate identity, the motion was rejected by five votes.

The British government then sought to overturn this vote with promises and propaganda, along with bribes and honours. When the motion came before the House again in 1800, the vote was 158 to 115 in favour of the motion. The Act of Union became law on 1 January 1801 and the Irish parliament was abolished.

▼ *British Prime Minister, William Pitt*

Act of Union

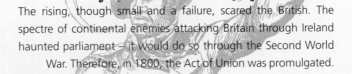

The rising, though small and a failure, scared the British. The spectre of continental enemies attacking Britain through Ireland haunted parliament – it would do so through the Second World War. Therefore, in 1800, the Act of Union was promulgated.

THE ACT ABOLISHED the Irish parliament and united Britain and Ireland into one kingdom with one parliament. As expected, the union inevitably lead to Great Britain's domination over her small, poor neighbour.

After the Act of Union, although Dublin continued to grow rapidly, it lost the gaiety and grandeur of a capital city. Many of those who had been members of the Irish parliament were now members at Westminster and had homes in London, rather than in Dublin.

The removal of the Irish parliament in itself did little to change the lives of the ordinary tenant farmers, since its members were mainly from the landed classes. They had legislated primarily to suit their own interests and not those of the people who worked on their estates.

▲ *A cartoon drawn in 1798*

What did make a big difference, though, was Westminster's power to pass coercion bills. These bills gave the government and the law enforcement agencies extraordinary powers of arrest, imprisonment and transportation; laws which were often enforced with injustice and cruelty. Often this was because the defendants had little understanding of the workings of the law, and sometimes they didn't speak enough English to understand the proceedings. In the northern counties, the local magistrates and juries were often Orangemen. Such was the extent of disquiet concerning the influence of the Orange Order that a parliamentary enquiry was set up in the 1830s to investigate the matter.

▲ *Members returning home from an Orange Day demonstration in the 1800s*

Emmet's Rising

1803 saw another attempted insurrection, involving some of those who had been involved in the 1798 rising, but this time it was led by a young Dublin Protestant, Robert Emmet.

T WAS A RATHER botched affair. Because of a fear of informers, insufficient information was passed to those who were to be involved, the result being short-lived chaos. Emmet had received a legacy from his father and with this he set about procuring and manufacturing arms.

On Saturday 23 July, Emmet went to lead his men and found that more men had come in from Kildare than he had been expecting. He didn't have sufficient weapons for even a small number of them and so,

▲ *Emmet preparing his followers for insurrection*

▲ *Emmet's supporters killing Lord Kilwarden*

disgruntled, many of them went away again. The rising was delayed until nine o'clock that evening, by which time most of them had gone home, under the impression that nothing was going to happen after all. Emmet had hoped to have 2,000 men when he led an attack on Dublin Castle, but in the end he had only 80.

The coach of the Chief Justice, Lord Kilwarden, happened to meet the mob in a narrow street and, after a confrontation, was attacked and the judge killed. Emmet realised that his attempt had failed and he called on those around him to disperse. The rising had lasted less than one day.

Emmet was captured about a month later and sentenced to be hanged, drawn and quartered. His speech from the dock has often been quoted, particularly the lines 'when my country has taken her place among the nations of the earth, then and not till then, let my epitaph be written'. Twenty-six of his associates were also executed.

Agrarian Disquiet

In rural areas of Ireland, various secret societies – such as Ribbonmen, Rockites, Molly Maguires and Caravats – flourished and organised sporadic campaigns of terror against landlords, their agents and their property. This was a sign of their frustration with a system that left so many small farmers and their families scarcely able to eke out a living.

THIS WAS THE ERA of the Napoleonic wars and creating a civil police force freed British soldiers from garrison duties, making them available for service on the Continent. Economic pressures forced thousands of Irishmen to join the British army and many fought and died at Waterloo in 1815. The war also increased economic prosperity, not for the small farmers but for the big producers of livestock and foodstuffs which were exported in large quantities to help the war effort. As many of the landowners, however, lived in England, the profits did not always find their way back into the Irish economy.

◀ *Cartoon depicting 'Captain Rock, Commander of the Insurgents in Ireland', dated 1822*

Protestants in the ruling and merchant classes tended to be Anglican, belonging to the Church of Ireland; but not all Protestants were wealthy. Many were farmers like the Catholics and a good number of these belonged to the Presbyterian Church, as their ancestors had frequently emigrated from Scotland. They too suffered from economic and political frustrations. Like Catholics, many had to sell the best and largest share of their crops to the landlords to pay their rent.

At the time of the Act of Union, influential Catholics had been led to believe that Catholic Emancipation (the full restoration of rights to Catholics) would follow the implementation of the act. This did not happen. It was some time before a new leader was to emerge who took a different approach to that of his predecessors.

▲ *Napoleon Bonaparte, against whom many Irishmen fought, and were killed, at Waterloo*

Daniel O'Connell

Daniel O'Connell (1775–1847) was a successful Kerry-born lawyer who had been educated in France.

I N THE CONTEXT OF European history, O'Connell is regarded as the most important politician among the subsequent adherents of what is classified as political Catholicism. At the same time he organised part of the Irish nation in a democratic mass campaign directed against the policy of the British government in the name of principles that every government claimed to uphold.

1822 was a year of extreme hardship and many starved in what was a precursor to the Great Famine of the 1840s. The plight of the small tenant farmers could no longer be ignored and relief committees were set up in many places.

The following year, 1823, O'Connell, with another lawyer, Richard Lalor Shiel, moved to form the Catholic Association, a group which had two main aims – to seek the repeal of the Penal Laws that still remained, and to improve the conditions endured by tenant farmers, hard-working men at the mercy of landlords who could charge them exorbitant rents and evict them at will.

The Association gathered what was known as 'the Catholic Rent' of one penny a week from its members to finance its operations. In this way, although it was led by lawyers, businessmen and the clergy, all the members felt that they were making a worthwhile contribution. It soon became a mass movement, with support among the poor and wealthy alike.

English cartoon of 1843 showing O'Connell with 'the Irish Frankenstein': the embodiment of the Repeal movement he created ▶

With a huge membership across the country it was able to exert pressure in a new way, a way that no group had done previously in Ireland, and O'Connell, a shrewd and courageous man, made sure that its activities remained lawful. It was Ireland's first experiment in democracy.

Catholic Emancipation

The Catholic Association scored its first major success in the general election of 1826, when its candidate was successful in County Waterford.

THE ASSOCIATION BACKED Villiers Stuart – a Protestant who supported its ideals – against George Beresford, a member of a prominent land-owning family in the area which had supplied the local member of parliament for over 70 years.

Despite the fact that the tenants on the Beresford estates were expected to vote for him (in an open public ballot), Beresford was defeated. There were similar successes in Louth, Monaghan and Westmeath. Encouraged by these successes, the Catholic Association realised that they would soon be in a position to challenge and defeat many of the anti-Emancipationist sitting MPs at the next general election.

In the end, they did not have to wait that long. In 1828, there was a bi-election in County Clare. Daniel O'Connell himself was chosen as candidate, and with the support of the best speakers in the Association and the help of the local Catholic clergy, he was elected with a majority of over 1,000 votes.

◀ *A 19th-century portrait of Daniel O'Connell by an unknown artist*

The prime minister, Arthur Wellesley, the Duke of Wellington, who had been born in Ireland and realised the danger of a mass revolt if change did not come about, pushed the Catholic Relief Bill through parliament. It became law on 13 April 1829. This removed nearly all of the institutionalised discrimination against Catholics within Ireland and Britain, with access now denied only to the highest offices of government and state.

The measure, however, was counterbalanced by a bill which abolished the voting rights of the 40-shilling freeholders, the small farmers, reducing the Irish electorate by 80 per cent, thus disenfranchising many of O'Connell's most loyal supporters.

▼ *The voting rights of small farmers were abolished*

The Cholera Epidemic and the Night of the Big Wind

In 1831–32, a cholera epidemic which had swept across Europe reached Ireland. It caused widespread panic and many deaths, especially as its cause was not understood and therefore not tackled. Another event, which had a major impact on the country in 1839, was an act of God.

6 JANUARY 1839 IS known as *Oiche na Gaoithe Moire*, or 'the Night of the Big Wind'. What appears to have been a hurricane, was the worst storm to hit Ireland in several centuries. It swept across the country causing great devastation and loss of life.

Mills, churches, great houses and cottages from Cork to Belfast were wrecked and thousands of trees were blown down. Such was the ferocity of the storm that many people thought that the end of the world had come. It made such an impression on people that despite

▲ *A religious illustration pleading for heavenly help against cholera* the upheaval caused by the Famine in the following decade it is an event which remains alive in the memory to this day.

▲ *The hurricane of 1839 laid waste many homes*

THE TITHE WAR

THE 1830s ALSO SAW many changes in Irish politics and society. Protestants and Catholics alike paid taxes amounting to 10 per cent of the produce of all tillage farming in tithes; these were paid to the local minister and became a major grievance.

Having successfully challenged the Protestant ascendancy's domination of parliament, the Catholic small farmers now turned their attention to the tithes, with a campaign which lasted until 1838 and became known as the Tithe War.

It began in Graignamanagh, County Kilkenny in 1831. Local people refused to pay the tithes, and despite the support of 600 soldiers and police, the minister went home empty-handed. There were many violent incidents and confrontations. One of the most serious of these happened near Fermoy, in County Cork, and has since become known as the 'massacre of Rathcormac'.

The Rev. Archdeacon Ryder wished to collect a tithe of four pounds and 16 shillings from a widow, Mrs. Ryan. In the ensuing struggle, nine people were killed, including the widow's son, and, amid the bloodshed, the soldiers seized four stacks of corn to meet the minister's demands.

Such actions only stiffened the resolve of those who were opposed to the tax and O'Connell, who was an opponent of the use of violence, continued to advocate passive resistance. These clashes also heightened sectarian tensions.

In 1838, the government reduced the tithes by 25 per cent and arranged that they would be collected by the landlord as an extra part of the rent and paid by him to the minister.

▼ *A meeting of the London School Board*

THE NATIONAL SCHOOLS SYSTEM

Other developments in the 1830s included the introduction of the National School System, which made primary education widely available. Based very much on the English syllabus and textbooks, it made no provision for education through the medium of Irish, which was still the language of the majority of the people in the country.

Indeed, it was often very hostile to the Irish language, with children frequently being punished and victimised for speaking their own tongue. These schools, together with the trauma of the Famine and the mass emigration it caused, were the two biggest factors in the decline of the use of the Irish language in the nineteenth century.

The Poor Law

The original aim of the Poor Law system was to provide indoor relief to the destitute poor in workhouses.

HOWEVER, AS A RESULT of the Great Famine, outdoor relief was granted in the form of money or goods to the able-bodied poor, and this ensured that by the turn of the century, the workhouses in Ireland had become a refuge for the old, sick and children under the age of 15.

In 1838, Ireland was divided into 137 unions; these had their basis in market towns where a workhouse or union house was built with an infirmary and fever hospital attached. At the time it was decided that an area with a radius of about 10 miles was the most suitable for administrative purposes. This system was financed by a rate collected under the Poor Law Valuation.

The Poor Law was introduced in 1836 to contend with the growing numbers of destitute people who had been forced off the land by high

▲ *Aerial view of a workhouse*

rents, crop failures, or simply because their holdings were so small that they were not economically viable.

Each union was to have its own workhouse which could accommodate up to 1,000 people. These grim places were little better than prisons. In 1844, before the onset of the Famine, 98 workhouses were already catering for 86,000 people, and when the time of crisis came, they were found to be totally inadequate. Men, women and children were segregated which meant that families were broken up.

The regimes and discipline were harsh and a lack of understanding of hygiene meant that disease and infestation were rife. The paupers were supposed to be gainfully employed, but often there was not enough work for them all. Many spent dull wasted lives behind the walls of these grim institutions.

▲ *Workhouses were grim, segregated, joyless places; little better than prisons*

Fr Mathew's Temperance Crusade

A more positive development, in 1838, was the founding of a mass temperance movement by Father Theobold Mathew, in response to the growing problem of alcohol abuse in the country. Many thousands of people took a pledge to abstain from intoxicating liquor.

SUCH WAS THE success of the movement that there was a noticeable decline in the number of faction fights at fairs and other incidents associated with over-indulgence in spirits, especially the illicitly-brewed *poitin* or *poteen* (an Irish word with the same origin as the English word 'potion').

Drunkenness had been a factor which undermined Robert Emmet's rising in 1803, yet when Daniel O'Connell held his great rallies in the 1840s, often serenaded by the local temperance bands, alcohol was not seen to have a detrimental effect on the behaviour of the assembled multitudes.

▲ *Father Theobold Mathew, leader of the Temperance movement*

DANIEL O'CONNELL'S MONSTER MEETINGS

BY 1840, DANIEL O'CONNELL felt that he had achieved all he could by lobbying at Westminster. He now took to the highways of Ireland, once more addressing huge meetings and exhorting the people to demand the repeal of the Union.

▲ *English cartoon depicting Daniel O'Connell as the king of Ireland*

By having these mass rallies, he was once more giving a voice and a role to the tens of thousands who had been disenfranchised in 1829. In 1843, a whole series of monster meetings was held, and while reports of attendances can at best be only very rough estimates, there is little doubt these were highly significant and very impressive occasions. It is reckoned that 120,000 came to hear him in Limerick, 150,000 in Kells, 300,000 in Cashel and estimates ranging from 750,000 to one million are given for the rally held at Tara in August of that year.

O'Connell well understood the historical significance of such places as Kells, Cashel and Tara. It is not surprising that he chose Clontarf as the location for the biggest rally, the one he hoped would break the hold of the outsider on Ireland in the same way that Brian Boru had defeated the Norsemen.

In the end, O'Connell succeeded in forcing the government to act, but not in the way that he had hoped. Instead they called his bluff and banned the meeting. A believer in the power of non-violent protest and fearing great loss of life, O'Connell called off the meeting and the British Army took control of Clontarf.

After this failure, O'Connell's career went into decline. As he reached his seventieth year his health also began to deteriorate. By the time of his death in 1847, Ireland was feeling the effects of the Famine and a new radical group had taken up the fight for Irish independence – the Young Irelanders.

Statue of Daniel O'Connell, in Dublin's O'Connell Street ▶

The Great Famine (*An Gorta Mor*)

The famine of 1845–49 was not the first famine in Ireland, but it was by far the most severe, persistent and widespread. Economic conditions for thousands of small farmers and their families had been precarious for many years. In hindsight, it is easy to see that there was a disaster waiting to happen.

THE POTATO HAD been introduced to Ireland at the end of the sixteenth century and its popularity grew because it was a crop well suited to Irish conditions, and one which produced a very high yield.

◄ *Despair as the potato crop fails*

A fungal blight, *phythphthora infestans*, was first noticed on potatoes in Ireland in 1845, having previously been recorded in the United States and Canada. About half the crop was affected. The following year, the failure was total and for the people who depended completely on the potato, the effect was catastrophic.

The workhouses, which were filled to capacity before the onset of the crisis, were unable to cope and many people were turned away from their doors. Soup kitchens were set up by local relief committees and by various religious organisations. The Quakers, in particular, won a place in the hearts of the Irish with their good work.

Others, however, were known to demand that Catholics become Protestants before receiving aid. Thus Catholics who became Protestants in the nineteenth century were described as having 'taken the soup', even if their conversion was not enforced by the famine. The government of the time, which did not believe in giving anyone anything for nothing, set up public works' schemes, where men, women and children were employed building roads and making other improvements.

▲ *Distributing alms to the needy at the height of the potato famine*

The Effect on the Country

If planted with potatoes, even a small farm could support a family. In other European countries, the presence of coal and iron had led to the spread of the Industrial Revolution and to the growth of cities and manufacturing industries.

THIS NEVER HAPPENED in Ireland, which had neither coal nor iron in significant quantities and so the vast majority of people continued to live off the land on small rented holdings.

The majority of Irish landlords, many of them absentees, cared little for the living conditions of their tenants as long as they got their rent, and very little of this money was re-invested in the Irish economy or even in their own estates, which were often heavily mortgaged.

At the same time, the Irish population was growing rapidly and appears to have doubled between 1800 and 1840; it may even have reached nine million by 1845. The country's present population is approximately 5,500,000.

The campaigns for Catholic emancipation and against tithes and the Act of Union were all related to the impoverished conditions endured by the small farmers. But these campaigns did little to improve their lot in the long run. Ireland wished to be self-governing so that it could tackle its own problems without British interests being taken into consideration.

▲ *A peasant family contemplating their meagre crop of potatoes*

The successes of Daniel O'Connell were too little and too late. In his final speech to the House of Commons, three months before his death in 1847, he was only too well aware of the proportions of the disaster which had befallen the country. His speech included the following words, 'Ireland is in your hands ... your power. If you do not save her she can't save herself.... I predict ... that one quarter of the population will perish unless you come to her relief'.

▼ *The majority of Ireland's poor depended on the land for their work*

Emigration to the US and Britain

Today, the sheer scale of the disaster of the famine is hard to grasp. At its peak, in August 1847, three million people a day attended soup kitchens. In the same year, 100,000 emigrated to Canada alone and in 1849 there were over 900,000 people being maintained in the workhouses which were maintained by local rate-payers.

THE EFFECTS OF the famine continued to be felt for decades afterwards, especially as the patterns of emigration established in the 1840s were maintained right through the century. It is estimated that four million people had left the country by 1900. This had a major impact, not only in Ireland but also in the United States, Canada and in British cities such as Glasgow and Liverpool, where large numbers of Irish settled in the post–famine period.

An Irish farmer contemplating his new life in America ▶

The many vessels that made the perilous journey across the Atlantic to the United States and Canada were often unseaworthy and grossly overcrowded. The impoverished emigrants were treated as a cargo rather than as passengers and often had to spend the entire voyage below deck. Because of the people's poor physical condition and the prevalence of disease among them, there were many deaths during these voyages and thus these vessels earned the nickname of 'coffin ships'.

People would cross the Atlantic any way they could and weren't at first concerned about the conditions in which they travelled. Ship owners and captains saw a chance to turn a quick buck on a trip that had been profitless just a few years before. The more unscrupulous among them got caught up in the profit margin.

The 'coffin ships' were born – scarcely seaworthy ships that sailed the Atlantic ridden with disease, short on provisions and long on people. Ships never designed for carrying any people were now laden with more passengers than they could safely carry. Some sank within a few days of leaving port.

▼ *An emigrant ship leaving Belfast Quay in 1851*

Those that crossed the Atlantic, arrived with their passengers more dead than alive. Some of the ships' names became notorious — a representation of the lack of concern of an imperial government that was doing less and less, it seemed, to protect its unwilling citizenry. *The Aeolus, The Lady Sale, The Looshtauk, The Elizabeth and Sarah,* all became famous through the death and disease they carried to British North America rather than through their sailing feats.

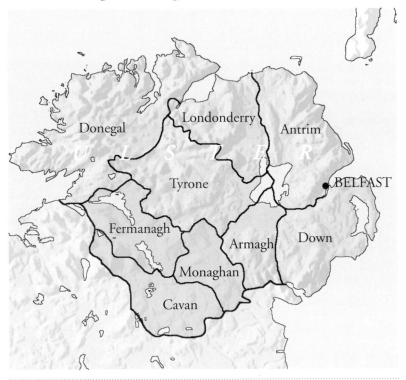

▲ *Up to 30 per cent of Ulster residents left for lives abroad in the mid-19th century*

The Ulster counties of Monaghan, Cavan and Fermanagh lost 30, 29 and 26 per cent respectively of their populations between 1841 and 1851, according to official census returns. Since the population had probably continued to increase up to at least 1845, the actual population loss may have been several per cent higher. Of the 26 per cent who were lost in Fermanagh, it is believed that about half of them died from hunger and disease and that the other half emigrated. The Fermanagh figures are quoted here as a reminder that the counties which now make up Northern Ireland were also badly affected by the failure of the potato crop.

Apart from the immediate loss of life, the Famine had several consequences that would have an effect on life in Ireland for the rest of the nineteenth century and beyond. It made emigration a fact of life in rural Ireland.

▲ *An 1881 illustration of Irish farm labourers travelling to England to find work*

Young Ireland and *The Nation*

In 1842, Thomas Davis, John Blake Dillon and Charles Gavan Duffy established *The Nation*, a newspaper which initially supported O'Connell in his repeal campaign by giving extensive coverage to his speeches. It also published many articles and poems on Irish historical themes, and it became very influential among the increasingly well-educated population.

AFTER THE DEFEAT of O'Connell's movement in 1843, the paper promoted a more radical approach placing itself within the republican tradition founded by Wolfe Tone and the other leaders of the 1798 rebellion.

Although Thomas Davis (1814–45) did not see the attempted revolt of 1848 – he died of scarletina three years before it. He was one of the most influential writers and ideologists of his generation, producing stirring ballads and well-argued essays. He had originally joined O'Connell's Repeal Association but soon decided that the spirit of Ireland as a nation needed to be awakened. Much of his writings deal with topics from Irish history. He hoped to motivate people with stories of past glories and tragedies.

▲ *The rebellion of 1798*

Charles Gavan Duffy (1816–1903) was a successful journalist originally from Monaghan. He brought his professional expertise to *The Nation*. Not a complete separatist, he would have been happy with some form of legislative independence from Britain. After the failure of the rising, he went to Australia, where he became active in politics, eventually becoming Prime Minister of Victoria in 1871.

Young Ireland grew out of the weekly *Nation*, a movement associated with Duffy and Thomas Davis (1814-45), a Protestant graduate of Trinity College, Dublin. Davis particularly admired the history of Jules Michelet, Augustin Thierry, and Jean de Sismondi. Although occasionally mentioned in *The Nation*, Mazzini had little impact on Davis and Duffy, who initially rejected the 'Young Ireland' tag, contrasting their brash immaturity with the proven statesmanship of O'Connell's Old Ireland.

▲ *Trinity College, Dublin*

Suppression and Transportation

Unlike O'Connell, the Young Irelanders were prepared to go on the offensive and, in1848, there was another failed uprising.

T WAS DAMAGED, as always, by the presence of informers and doomed to failure in any case because of a lack of preparation and, more importantly, because the spirit of the people had already been broken by the Famine. By this time, hundreds of thousands of people were dying of starvation and disease. The only major confrontation was at Ballingarry, County Tipperary, where the rebels (the leaders of whom included Catholics and Protestants) were soon defeated by the police.

Other important leaders of this movement were William Smith O'Brien and Thomas Meagher, both of whom were transported to Van Dieman's Land (now Tasmania), and John Mitchel, who was gaoled for five years. O'Brien and Meagher were eventually joined in Tasmania by Mitchel and two other Young Ireland editors. Four of them later escaped to America. O'Brien – a better martyr than an insurgent leader – and his two remaining colleagues were released in 1854 and returned to Ireland in 1856. Refusing to return to parliament, O'Brien lived quietly until his death in 1864.

▲ *Daniel O'Connell, the inspiration for later leaders such as O'Brien and Meagher*

Though O'Brien and other Young Irelanders later admitted that their rising in July 1848 had been a mistake, several of the participants, though not O'Brien himself, later joined the new Fenian movement. 1848 has thus been incorporated into an Irish patriotic tradition of revolt leading to the Anglo-Irish War of 1919-21.

The greatest legacy of the Young Irelanders is the amount of patriotic literature they produced, ranging from Mitchel's *Jail Journal* to rousing popular ballads, which are still sung to this day. In helping to promote and define Irish nationalism, the Young Irelanders were to be an inspiration for many Irish nationalists of future generations.

▲ *A Fenian arms factory discovered in Birmingham, England*

The Fenian Movement

The influence of Young Ireland and the repeal movement swelled into the United States as thousands of immigrants fled the famine of their homeland. In America, two leaders emerged who would pioneer the Fenian uprisings: James Stephens and John O'Mahoney.

BOTH OF THESE MEN found enough anti-English feelings in the States to lead them to believe that a revolt among Irish-Americans was entirely possible. O'Mahoney spearheaded the Fenian organisation, which was also known as the Irish Republican Brotherhood, a secret oath-bound society dedicated to armed revolution. The alliance was suppressed, but it remained active and gave birth to a new generation of revolutionary Fenians.

Stephens and O'Mahony had been leaders of the Young Ireland movement who had gone to Paris in 1848, after the failure of their uprising, and found France in a state of revolution. They proceeded to America, with the republican ideas they had encountered in France, and met up with former comrades there. More militant than

▲ *Many emigrants were Fenian supporters, this led to the idea of an Irish-American revolution*

before, they published their own newspapers and kept Irish America informed on the developing situation in Ireland. Their material was strongly anti-English in tone and was avidly read in Ireland and the States.

When Stephens returned to gauge the situation and the mood in Ireland at first hand, he met up with Jeremiah O'Donovan Rossa, who had formed the Phoenix National and Literary Society. This group had branches in various parts of the country but did not become a political movement until it joined forces with the Irish-Americans, thereby becoming the Irish Republican Brotherhood in 1858. On the suggestion of O'Mahoney, in New York, they became known as the Fenians.

The misery caused by the potato famine led to fervent anti-English activities ▶

The Fenians and the Funeral of Terence Bellew McManus

The Fenian movement started demonstrations, organised financial backing and led armed insurrections, all in the effort to end British rule.

AFTER MANY SPEECHES, marches, picnics and conferences, the Fenians made good on their words of invasion, especially in the USA. The most famous series of these raids were led across the American border into the Canadian frontier.

Members of the Fenian movement swore allegiance to the Irish Republic 'now virtually established'. They were committed to the complete separation of Ireland from England and were prepared to use physical force to achieve this goal. They regarded themselves as the revolutionary heirs of Wolfe Tone.

A significant event in 1861 was the reburial in Dublin of Terence Bellew McManus (1812–61). Born in County Fermanagh, he attended school in Monaghan with Charles Gavan Duffy. Moving to Liverpool, he became a very prosperous businessman and also a prominent member of the

Wolfe Tone, an inspirational revolutionary ▲

repeal campaign in the city. He intended travelling to Clontarf to O'Connell's monster meeting there in 1843. However, the Liverpool delegation was prevented from travelling when the government requisitioned the ferries to bring in extra troops. By the time McManus arrived in Dublin, the meeting had been called off.

He moved to Ireland, taking part in the action at Ballingarry – for this he was arrested in Cork harbour. Originally sentenced to death, his sentence was commuted to transportation to Tasmania. He escaped from there in 1852 and made his way to America; settling in San Francisco, where he died in 1861. His body was returned to Ireland where a huge crowd followed his coffin to the grave. Here, by reminding people of the earlier revolt, the Fenians helped to rekindle Irish political aspirations.

▲ *Cartoon of Irish farmers bringing their goods to 'King O'Connell'*

The Fenian Rising

A rising was planned for 1867, but because of the arrest of many of the leaders, the actions were sporadic and ineffective. Originally planned for 11 February, it was postponed.

WORD OF THE postponement never got to Kerry or England, and actions went ahead with little success. The following month there was limited action in Clare, Cork, Limerick and Tipperary, but these were quickly and vigorously dealt with by the authorities.

THE MANCHESTER MARTYRS

THE MOST SIGNIFICANT events took place in England later in the year. In September 1867, two Fenian leaders were arrested and brought to Manchester for trial. On their way to the court, the prison van was stopped by a large group of Fenians, who attempted to break it open. When the use of stones and a hatchet failed, someone shot the lock off, unfortunately mortally wounding a policeman

▲ *A cartoon of 1867, depicting a Fenian dragon slaying St George*

inside the van. The prisoners and their rescuers then escaped.

After the policeman's death, a widespread manhunt was launched and many were arrested. Three were eventually tried and sentenced to death. William Philip Allen, Michael Larkin and Michael O'Brien – who were innocent of the crime – were hanged on 23 November 1867, instantly becoming known as the 'Manchester Martyrs'. Their deaths caused great bitterness and resentment among the Irish at home and in America, undoubtedly strengthening a movement that had not been very significant up to that time.

Another attempt at rescuing Fenian prisoners in England had disastrous consequences. An explosive charge was placed against the wall of the Clerkenwell Detention Centre. It exploded, killing 12 people instantly and fatally wounding another 18. This provoked a furious reaction from the British parliament and press. A Fermanagh-born Fenian, Michael Barratt, was executed for his part in this event and was the last person to be publicly hanged in England.

▼ *The Fenian explosion at Clerkenwell, 1868*

The Disestablishment of the Church of Ireland

The Reformed Presbyterian Church of Ireland has its immediate roots in the Second Scottish Reformation (1638–49). After periods of struggle and persecution, the first Irish Reformed Presbytery was set up through the work of Scottish Covenanters in 1763. The first Synod met in 1811.

IN 1869, WILLIAM GLADSTONE made his first significant contribution to Irish affairs with his Church Disestablishment Act. Prior to this, the Church of Ireland had been the official church, but now the legal connection between the Church and the State was severed. Gladstone had first proposed the motion while in opposition in 1868 and forced a general election on the issue. This election brought him to power as prime minister. Once appointed, he was able to guide the bill through parliament.

This did not mean the end of the hated tithes, but it was regarded by many people in Ireland as being highly significant, for it was seen as a recognition of the dwindling importance of the old

▲ *Prime Minister, William Gladstone*

Protestant ascendancy. Also significant was the option given to tenants of church lands to buy out their properties using mortgages arranged under terms stipulated in the Act. Within 10 years, about three quarters of glebe tenants had availed themselves of the opportunity to purchase their holdings, and thus a model had been established which was to prove useful when later land-purchase schemes were being formulated.

By 1870, the situation in which many small farmers found themselves in was still intolerable, and political debate centred on whether the British government could be forced to introduce significant reforms or whether an Irish parliament would be required if the necessary changes were to be achieved.

▲ *At first, Gladstone's reforms did little to ease the plight of the small farmers*

The Home Rule League and Isaac Butt

Isaac Butt (1815–79), the son of a Church of Ireland minister in County Donegal, founded the Home Rule Association in 1870 with the aim of establishing an Irish parliament, which would have full control over domestic affairs.

I N THE 1874 general election, his party won more than half the Irish seats at Westminster, helped no doubt by the fact that this was the first election where the secret ballot was used. Previously, voters had had to declare their preferences in public, meaning they were under tremendous peer pressure to vote a certain way.

Butt's party initially made little impact in government because it did not hold the balance of power. However, by using filibuster – the delaying of parliamentary progress by methods such as making deliberately extended speeches – and other obstructionist tactics. It often caused considerable disruption to parliamentary procedures, keeping Irish issues to the fore.

An illustration of Isaac Butt, from an 1873 edition of Vanity Fair ▲

Under Butt's leadership the party was very disjointed: it lacked unity in ideas, organisation and membership. It has been argued that he lacked the singlemindedness or ruthlessness necessary to make an impact on the political system. The party was split into three separate groups: genuine Home Rulers with beliefs similar to Butt; Fenians; and crypto-Liberals who had joined in order to ensure victory in the elections. Despite its differences, however, the Home Rule Party was instrumental in focusing Irish minds on achieving their own government. Once again, the determination to break free of English rule was reinforced.

In 1879, Butt was succeeded as leader of the Home Rule Party by Charles Stewart Parnell (1845–91), also a Protestant.

▼ *Parnell addressing an anti-rent meeting in Limerick, 1879*

Charles Stewart Parnell

The great Irish statesman, Charles Stewart Parnell, was born at Avondale, County Wicklow. He was educated at, and graduated from, Magdalene College, in Cambridge, England.

PARNELL WAS MADE high sheriff of Wicklow in 1874, and the following year was sent to parliament in Meath; from which county he was returned for three constituencies.

In 1879, Parnell was elected president of the Irish National Land League, in the formation of which he had taken part; the object of the League was the reduction of rents, and to facilitate the obtaining of the ownership of the soil by the occupiers.

In 1880, Parnell visited the United States. Lecturing in all the principal cities, he also addressed the house of representatives at Washington. The result of his visit created a feeling which crystallised itself in the formation of the Grand League Associations, which have proved the main financial support of the home organisation.

▲ *A portrait engraving of Charles Stewart Parnell*

Parnell had been twice arrested for his connection with the Land League, which had been declared illegal. The jury disagreed on the first trial, and he was discharged. However his second arrest, in October 1881, was more successful. He was convicted and sent to Kilmainham gaol. From where he was released in the following May.

Parnell's policy in the leadership of his party, had been to obstruct business in the House of Commons and, with the Home Rule question, to create an agitation against the high rents paid by the Irish tenantry. In this way, he united the common people of Ireland on his side, and made it impossible for the English to ignore Ireland's demand for Home Rule.

▲ *Parnell and Dillon in gaol*

Michael Davitt and the Land League

Around the same time as Parnell was making an impression in parliament, a young reformer named Michael Davitt (1846–1906) had returned to Ireland from America; there he had gained the support of many Irish-Americans for a new land reform campaign.

THE WINTER OF 1878-79 had been particularly severe. Once again, the spectre of famine loomed across Ireland, especially in the poorer counties of the west where many faced eviction and starvation. In April 1879 in County Mayo, Davitt had organised a very successful protest which prevented the eviction of tenants, who had been unable to pay their rents, from an estate in Irishtown.

Before long Davitt realised the advantage there would be in working with both Parnell's party and the American Fenians, who now called themselves *Clan na Gael*. By bringing together these three strands of Irish political opinion – land-reformers, home-rulers and republicans – he created a broad coalition with mutually compatible aims that had wide support across the country. Both Davitt and Parnell became very popular national figures. It was a sign of their mutual respect that they were prepared to work so closely together.

Davitt had previously served seven years in an English gaol for Fenian activities. Being the son of a small farmer from County Mayo who had been evicted for non-payment of rent and forced to emigrate to England, Michael wished to change forever the landlord-tenant relationship as it existed in Ireland.

As 1879 progressed, however, it was the land issue which became the most pressing, as more and more farmers found themselves in difficulty with crop failures and unpaid rent. In October, Davitt founded the Irish National Land League and Parnell became its first president. Because the League had strong financial backing from the United States and the support of the Catholic hierarchy and clergy at home, it proved very effective in getting its message across. It publicised the evils of the landlord system as it then pertained, and gave relief to those who faced, or had already suffered, eviction.

▲ *Land League supporters demonstrate at a forced sale of cattle (taken in lieu of rent)*

The Origins of 'Boycott'

The Land League organised demonstrations and rallies as well as using other non-violent tactics, such as the boycott, to pressurise the landlords and the government.

T WAS THE LEAGUE'S actions against Captain Charles Boycott in County Mayo – who was forced to bring in Orangemen from Cavan and Fermanagh to harvest Lord Erne's crops, something no local person would do – that led to Boycott's name being given to that action it now signifies in any English dictionary. Although the League did not advocate the use of violence, there were many incidents which brought death and destruction on all sides.

▲ *Troops protect Captain Charles Boycott as he gathers in his harvest*

▲ *Police charge into a Land League demonstration in Limerick*

UNREST IN THE COUNTRY

AS THE COUNTRYSIDE SLID towards anarchy, the government responded in 1881 by arresting Parnell and instantly making him a national hero. Many leaders of the Land League were also arrested and the campaign was intensified. Gladstone had passed a Land Act in 1881 which did not go far enough towards solving the problem and now he negotiated what was called the Treaty of Kilmainham (the name of the gaol) with Parnell. Parnell was to be released in return for using his influence to end the land war.

The Phoenix Park Murders

Almost immediately, however, hopes of progress in the discussions between Parnell, the Land League and the government were shattered by the murders, in Phoenix Park, Dublin, of the newly arrived Chief Secretary, Lord Frederick Cavendish and the Under Secretary, T. H. Burke.

AGROUP CALLING ITSELF the 'Invincibles', which was opposed to any negotiations with Britain, claimed responsibility. The government responded by introducing a new coercion act. Parnell survived the crisis and a subsequent attempt to implicate him in the killings using forged diaries. He even won libel damages against the *Times*.

Despite the Phoenix Park murders, Gladstone pressed ahead with land reforms. In 1881, he introduced a Land Act which guaranteed the 'Three Fs': fair rent, fixity of tenure and free sale. These had been among the main demands of the Land League. The Act also ensured that any improvements made by tenants would not lead to rent increases, as in the past.

The process of the transfer of land ownership,

◀ *Fenians assassinate English officials, Cavendish and Burke, in Phoenix Park*

which had been initiated by the Church Disestablishment Act of 1869, was continued by Lord Ashbourne's Purchase of Land Act of 1885, which allowed for the purchase of nearly one million acres of land by tenants using government loans.

George Wyndham's Land Act of 1903 more or less completed the process, providing the Land Commission with money to purchase estates. These, in turn, were sold to the tenants on terms of 68 years repayments. The terms of this Act had been agreed by leaders of the Land League, the Irish Parliamentary Party and the government, at a conference in 1902.

Interestingly, Wyndham was a great-grandson of Lord Edward Fitzgerald, and Lord Ashbourne was the grandson of a prominent United Irishman in County Cavan.

▲ *An 1888 cartoon,* 'The Times *corners Parnell'*

Gladstone's Home Rule Bill

The success of the Irish party in the 1885 election meant that they held the balance of power in the new parliament, and the following year Gladstone brought forward his first Home Rule Bill.

THIS BILL OFFERED only partial devolution of powers to a Dublin parliament, but despite this, it was defeated on its second reading. It also led to rioting in Belfast, claiming at least 30 lives.

There were a number of reasons for Gladstone having such difficulty in solving the Irish problem. These included opposition from within the Commons and the Lords, from the Conservative Party, from Gladstone's own Liberal Party, and also from the majority of the English electorate.

On top of this, there was the massive problem of the complexity of the Irish Question in attempting to reach a suitable compromise,

▲ *A portrait of Gladstone as an old man, in his study*

the unfortunate circumstances from which Gladstone attempted to tackle the question and also the added problem of the Ulster Unionists. Even before the introduction of the first Home Rule Bill, there was a small minority of Liberals voting with the Conservatives in an attempt to prevent Gladstone from introducing Home Rule.

When Gladstone's sense of morality forced him to believe that in order to achieve 'justice for Ireland' it, as a country 'rightly struggling to be free', deserved Home Rule, he kept it private because he feared the massive opposition he knew that such a bombshell would incite. One of the major reasons for him keeping this private was his realisation that it would result in a serious split in the Liberal Party – this was one of the most important factors in preventing Gladstone from bringing Home Rule to Ireland.

▲ *Cartoon of 1893 depicting Gladstone as a pilgrim walking the Home Rule wall*

The Northern Situation

In the north-east, 1859 had been the 'year of grace', a year of religious fanaticism which had seen a marked revival of fundamental Protestantism, in turn leading to increased sectarian tensions.

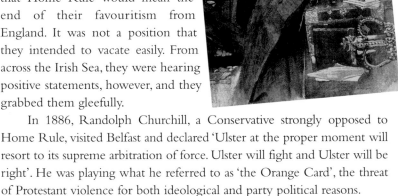

FROM TIME TO TIME, this erupted into serious violence, and politicians were not slow to use this to their own advantage, warning of dire consequences if unpopular measures were passed. The Protestant population feared that Home Rule would mean the end of their favouritism from England. It was not a position that they intended to vacate easily. From across the Irish Sea, they were hearing positive statements, however, and they grabbed them gleefully.

In 1886, Randolph Churchill, a Conservative strongly opposed to Home Rule, visited Belfast and declared 'Ulster at the proper moment will resort to its supreme arbitration of force. Ulster will fight and Ulster will be right'. He was playing what he referred to as 'the Orange Card', the threat of Protestant violence for both ideological and party political reasons.

▲ *Gladstone introducing his Home Rule bill in the House of Commons*

A few months later, in the General Election, Gladstone and the Liberal Party, which had split on the issue of Home Rule, were defeated and the Conservatives under Lord Salisbury took office.

'Home Rule means Rome Rule' was a slogan that emerged at this time, playing on Protestant fears that an Irish parliament would be dominated by Catholics and that such a parliament would choose to persecute Protestants. It should be remembered, however, that many of the leaders of the main Irish political movements of the nineteenth century, such as Tone, Emmet, Davis, Butt and Parnell, were themselves Protestants.

▼ *Cartoon depicting Gladstone and Salisbury (General Election, July 1886)*

The Downfall of Parnell

In opposition, Gladstone and Parnell continued to work towards achieving Home Rule for Ireland. Parnell was suspicious of concessions made by the Conservative government, fearing that they were attempting to 'kill Home Rule by kindness'.

N THE END, however, Parnell was the author of his own downfall. For many years, he had been having an affair with Katharine O'Shea, wife of the Captain O'Shea he had chosen as candidate for the 1886 Galway bi-election. Eventually, Captain O'Shea filed for divorce at Christmas 1889, naming Parnell as co-respondent.

Both Gladstone and the Catholic Church now felt that Parnell was a liability to the Home Rule cause and began to pressure him into resigning as leader of the party. By refusing to do so Parnell split the party from top to bottom. He died in

▲ *An 1880 cartoon depicting Gladstone and Parnell making pancakes together*

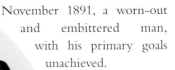

November 1891, a worn-out and embittered man, with his primary goals unachieved.

His funeral was perhaps the greatest spectacle Dublin had ever witnessed. An estimated 200,000 Irishmen – both Catholic and Protestant – stood in the pouring rain as the coffin passed by. Six abreast they walked, moving slowly to the strains of 'The Death March' from Handel's *Saul*. The sea of black mourning clothes was punctuated only by the green armbands of the mourners, and the glint of brass from the instruments of the 30 bands that filled the streets.

As the funeral cortege, followed by Parnell's riderless horse, wove its way through the Irish capital's wet and muddy streets, the crowd stopped at the consecrated memorials to those other men who had fought for Ireland. At each stop, more mourners joined the throng. A Dublin paper reported that it took the funeral procession three hours to pass any given spot. Dozens fainted when they saw his casket.

▲ Punch *illustration showing Gladstone breaking with Parnell after the O'Shea case*

The Second Home Rule Bill

In the July 1893 election, Gladstone, at the age of 83, was returned to power for his fourth term as prime minister with the support of the Irish Party MPs. Early the following year he introduced his second Home Rule Bill which was, once again, fiercely debated.

DESPITE THREATS FROM the Unionists at their 1892 conference, William Gladstone introduced the Second Home Rule Bill in 1893. In a victorious vote, it was passed by the House of Commons. However it was defeated in the UK's upper house (the House of Lords), where there were many more Conservatives than Liberals: a Bill can't become law in Britain unless both Houses pass it.

Gladstone resigned as prime minister the following year and the Liberal government itself quit in 1895. In the General Election, the Conservatives and Unionists gained a majority of over 150 and were to remain in power for over a decade.

The nineteenth century had witnessed the growth of conscious

◀ *The hearing of Gladstone's Second Home Rule Bill*

separatism between Ulster and the rest of Ireland. The effects of the industrial revolution in Ireland were confined almost entirely to the northern part of the country, strapping even closer its industrial and commercial dependency on Britain. The greater prosperity of the north and its economic structure increased its alienation from the rest of Ireland.

▲ *While the north prospered from industry, the south remained impoverished*

As Ireland entered the twentieth century, and with the Conservatives in power and the Irish Party in disarray following the Parnell split, the prospects for Home Rule in the foreseeable future seemed bleak. Other developments in Ireland, however, were to prove significant.

The Unionists and Northern Ireland

In the 1890s, as the pressure for Irish Home Rule increased, Irish
Protestants who supported the union with Britain felt threatened
and saw the need for some sort of formal unionist organisation.

AS A RESULT OF THIS, unionist clubs were formed all over Ireland. In December 1904, a meeting of Ulster Unionists was held in Belfast and the following resolutions were adopted as a result: an Ulster Unionist Council should be formed; and an Ulster Union should bring into line all local unionist associations in the province of Ulster with a view to consistent and continuous political action.

At a meeting in the Ulster Hall, Belfast on 3 March 1905, under the chairmanship of Colonel James McCalmont, MP for East Antrim, the Ulster Unionist Council was formally constituted. The Council consisted of about 200 members.

This would be a precursor to the active efforts instigated by Carson early in the twentieth century to secure Ireland's place within the union with Britain. When Carson retired as Unionist leader due to age and ill-health, he was replaced by Sir James Craig who, unlike the Dublin-born Carson, was quite happy to see the north being dealt with on a separate basis.

Craig became prime minister of Northern Ireland when the unionists took 40 of the 52 seats in the northern parliament. Sinn Fein took six. Under the Government of Ireland Act 1920, the northern and southern parts of Ireland were to have the same constitutional basis and relationship with the British government and there was scope for the development of north-south bodies to deal with matters of mutual interest.

◀ *An Orange Order march near Portadown*

▲ *Sir James Craig freely allowed northern and southern Ireland to function separately*

The Gaelic Athletic Association

The Gaelic Athletic Association (GAA) was founded in 1884 to promote traditional Irish sports and it soon became a nationwide movement with teams, clubs and tournaments organised on a parish, county and all-Ireland basis.

THE ASSOCIATION'S founders, Michael Cusack and Maurice Davin, wanted to preserve and cultivate their country's national games. To this day the GAA remains an amateur organisation. When it was founded, Davin was created the first president and Dr T. W. Croke, (Archbishop of Cashel) was its first patron. Croke Park in Dublin (the Association Headquarters) is named in his honour.

The Association was nationalist in outlook and members were banned from playing non-Gaelic games. The Association also banned members of British Crown Forces from membership – something that is a source of great controversy in modern-day Ireland. Foreign games are also banned from GAA stadiums. The GAA is the largest sporting organisation in Ireland, boasting 2,800 clubs comprising of 182,000 footballers and 97,000 hurlers. Membership of the GAA exceeds 800,000 at home and

▲ *A hurling game in Kilkenny*

abroad, ensuring its role as a powerful national movement with an important social and cultural influence in Irish life.

Like all sports, the GAA is proud of its own records. The highest attendance ever recorded at an All-Ireland Senior Football Final was 90,556 at the 1961 Down vs Offaly Final. Following the introduction of seating to the Cusack stand in 1966, the largest crowd recorded was reduced to 73,588. The highest number of appearances in the All-Ireland Senior Football final is 10. This has been achieved by Paudie O'Shea, Pat Spillane and Denis 'Ogie' Moran. They were winners on no less than eight occasions. The highest individual score in the modern 70-minute game was recorded by Jimmy Keaveney (Dublin) in the 1977 Final against Armagh where he scored two goals and six points (12 points), and by Mike Sheehy (Kerry) in the 1979 Final against Dublin where he also recorded 2-6.

▲ *Non-Gaelic sports, such as polo, are banned from all GAA stadiums*

The Gaelic League

The Gaelic League, which was founded in 1893 by Douglas Hyde and Eoin MacNeill, aimed to promote the Irish language. They had seen that the language had gone into decline since the famine and was further depleted by the ongoing emigration.

TOGETHER, THE GAA and the Gaelic League raised the consciousness among ordinary people across the country of what it meant to be Irish. Both organisations were also implicitly separatist in that they stressed that Ireland was a different country, with a different culture, and not merely an English province or colony. This cultural nationalism took many forms and engaged the minds of many of the new

generation of writers and poets writing in both English and Irish.

The Gaelic League also popularised 'Irish' entertainments such as fiddling, piping, dancing, reciting poetry and listening to lectures. Douglas Hyde was elected to be the president and stayed in office in that position for 22 years.

The census of 1851 showed 319,602 persons whose sole language was Gaelic, and 1,204,684 who spoke some Gaelic (perhaps only a few words) in addition to English; by 1891, the respective figures were 38,192 and 642,053. The numbers were decreasing drastically and the founding members found this to be disturbing, so they made it their mission to correct it.

The League's original aims were: the preservation of Irish as the national language of the country and the extension of its use as the spoken tongue; the study and publication of existing Gaelic literature, and the cultivation of a modern literature in Irish.

◀ *Traditional Irish dancers*   *A Gaelic Post Office sign, in Dingle, Kerry* ▲

Anglo-Irish Literature

Around this time, there was also an Anglo-Irish literary revival which brought writers such as William Butler Yeats, Lady Gregory and John Millington Synge to the fore. As the term 'Anglo-Irish' implies, this literature was largely the preserve of the remains of the ascendancy class.

Often the works of these writers were a voyage of discovery into Ireland's ancient and heroic past. They were consciously choosing to see themselves as Irish and to weave another strand into the cultural tapestry of the country rather than to remain aloof and try to be British. Many of their books, poems and plays became popular at home and abroad and Yeats went on to win the Nobel Prize for literature in 1923.

The poetry and writings of William Butler Yeats were a display of his passion for mysticism and the Occult Sciences. His is one of the many famous names to come from the original Golden Dawn. His works include such titles as *Your Pathway* and 'Never Give All The Heart'. However, more important was his desire and striving for knowledge of the unknown; that which beyond human knowledge.

Many writers were attracted by the rich speech patterns of the country people and they used as their models the remnants of the Gaelic traditions which these people had carried with them into English. Some, such as Synge, even went so far as to learn Irish so that he could tap directly into this deep vein of culture and tradition that lay just below the surface, despite centuries of repression.

All these cultural movements helped to reawaken the national spirit which had lain dormant since the dark days of the famine. They also encouraged debate and helped to create a new positive national identity.

▲ *The Isle of Innisfree, County Sligo, which inspired Yeats to write 'The Lake Isle of Innisfree'*

The Events of 1898

1898 saw the passing of the Local Government Act, which set up county councils and did away with the old Grand Jury system that had been dominated by the landlords and their supporters.

THIS WAS A significant move – democracy had finally been brought closer to the ordinary people, giving them an opportunity to influence developments within their own localities. The dominance of the landlord over local affairs had been removed at last.

1898 also marked the centenary of the 1798 rebellion and the widespread commemorations of the event revived a lot of interest in the personalities and ideologies of that time.

In particular, the memory of Wolfe Tone was evoked. His message to Ireland and the Irish was remembered: 'To subvert the tyranny of our execrable government, to break the connection with England, the never failing source of all our political evils, and to assert the independence of my country, these were my objects. To unite the whole people of Ireland, to abolish the memory of past dissentions, and to substitute the common name of Irishman in place of the denominations of Protestant, Catholic, and Dissenter; these were my means.'

Wolfe Tone ▶

ARTHUR GRIFFITH & SINN FEIN

In South Africa, Arthur Griffith, a Dublin-born printer, helped the Irish Transvaal Society to organise a celebration and the following year he returned to Dublin to found a newspaper called the 'United Irishman' in which he praised the ideals of the rebels of 1798, 1848 and 1867.

He did not believe that any action taken by the Irish MPs at Westminster would bring about change in Ireland. He believed that the Irish needed to work on their own and set up their own institutions and structures and that the Irish MPs should set up their own parliament in Dublin. He wished to see English institutions replaced by Irish ones, an idea which ran parallel with Douglas Hyde's call for the de-Anglicisation of Ireland, one which Griffith would develop in 1905 into a movement called *Sinn Fein*, which translates as 'we ourselves', or 'just us'.

▲ *Sinn Fein's logo*

The Liberals Return to Power

By 1900, the Irish Party had regrouped under John Redmond's leadership and recovered the support it had lost because of the Parnell scandal and split. However, they had to wait until the 1906 election and the defeat of the Conservatives before they could hope to see any progress towards the granting of Home Rule.

BY 1910, THE LIBERALS had curbed the powers of the House of Lords, but had lost their overall majority in the process. This meant that they were now dependent on the Irish Party MPs. They knew that the Lords could now no longer block the implementation of a Bill passed by the House of Commons. Thus, when the Home Rule Bill was passed in the Commons in 1912, this appeared to be a major triumph for John Redmond

A heavily guarded march by Orangemen ▶

and his party. They believed that Home Rule would become a reality within two years. A rapidly changing situation in Ireland and on the Continent, however, brought unforeseen results.

THE ORANGE ORDER IS REVIVED

THE UNIONISTS IN THE NORTH OF IRELAND had been reacting for some time to the changing political scene. The Orange Order had been revitalised in 1866. In 1890 celebrations of the bi-centenary of the Battle of the Boyne of 12 July 1690 had a similar effect on Unionist hearts and minds as the commemorations of 1798 were to have on nationalists and republicans in 1898.

Once again, the traditions of Protestantism came to the fore. The Battle of the Boyne was once again adapted as a focus for their heritage. Unionists were determined that history would not be undermined, no matter what negotiations were going on behind closed doors in Dublin and London. They were suspicious of anybody who talked to the native Irish about Home Rule.

William III at the Battle of the Boyne ▶

Carson Against Home Rule

Sir Edward Carson (1854–1935), a Dublin-born lawyer, was a Unionist member of parliament for Dublin University from 1892–1918.

HE HELD A NUMBER OF significant positions in Ireland and Britain: Solicitor General for Ireland (1900–05); Attorney General in Britain (1915); First Lord of the Admiralty (1916); and later he was also a member of the war cabinet. From 1918, he sat for a Belfast constituency.

Leader of the Unionist Party from 1910, he was a prominent organiser of the campaign against Home Rule, especially the Ulster Volunteers. Although he was offered the position of prime minister when the Northern Ireland parliament was established, he turned it down on the grounds that partition was a defeat for unionism. He believed vehemently that the whole of Ireland should have remained part of the United Kingdom.

◀ *Propaganda from the time of the Home Rule campaigns*

Sir Edward Carson speaking against Home Rule in Belfast ▶

THE BELFAST RALLIES

Carson became leader of the Unionist party in 1910 and saw opposition to Home Rule as a way of keeping all of Ireland within the Union. He encouraged protestations of unionism in the North as a way of preventing Home Rule for Ireland, rather than as a demand for separate treatment for the Protestant people of the north-east.

When he visited Belfast in 1911, he told a huge audience that Home Rule would be resisted, and that if the Bill became law, the Unionist MPs would set up a government for the province of Ulster (nine counties). Within a few days of this speech, a committee had been set up to draft an Ulster constitution.

Carson believed that Redmond would not accept Home Rule for part of the country only, and that if Ulster opposition was strong enough, the whole scheme would have to be abandoned. The Conservative Party, especially under Bonar Law, who became its leader at the end of 1911, sided strongly with the unionists. They saw Home Rule both as a threat to the empire and to the interests of the British landed classes, many of whom still retained property in Ireland.

By January 1912, the unionists were openly organising a large military force, the Ulster Volunteer Force (UVF). After nine months of these preparations, a mass meeting was called in Belfast on 28 September and a petition, the 'Ulster Solemn League and Covenant', was launched, which was to be signed by over 200,000 people across the north. They pledged themselves to use 'all means which may be necessary to defeat the present conspiracy to set up a Home Rule parliament in Ireland'.

▲ *Crowds arriving at City Hall for the signing of the Ulster Covenant*

When they spoke of Ulster, they meant the nine-county province. Although they spoke of a Protestant Ulster standing firm against Home Rule, the fact of the matter was that Catholics made up close to half of the population and that they had a majority (albeit a small one in Fermanagh and Tyrone) in five of those nine counties.

THE TITANIC DISASTER

THE OTHER STORY THAT DOMINATED the news in Belfast in 1912 was the sinking of the Titanic, a ship that had been built at the Harland and Wolff shipyard in the city. The huge luxury liner had hit an iceberg on her maiden voyage across the Atlantic, with 1,400 people killed in the icy waters.

White Star triple-screw steamer "Titanic", 45,000 tons, which sank on April 15th 1912 with 1635 people.

▲ *The ocean liner* Titanic — *once believed to be unsinkable*

Home Rule

Northern Ireland came into existence as a result of a campaign for Irish Home Rule, begun in the 1870s. At that time, the whole island of Ireland was governed by Britain and their MPs were sent to Westminster – the home of the British Government in London.

HOME RULERS WANTED a separate Irish parliament, but their campaign was defeated by a number of groups, including Irish unionists, who wanted to remain under British rule.

Irish politician John Redmond faced the same opposition when he forced the issue again in 1911. Under the leadership of Sir Edward Carson, thousands of unionists signed the 'Ulster Solemn League and Covenant' on 28 September 1912, opposing the Home Rule Bill and reaffirming Protestant support for the union with Britain.

Declaring in the House of Commons that he regarded the Bill as 'very much more a British than an Irish question', Carson condemned the sacrifice of the essential interests of the empire and of the United Kingdom as a whole by politicians who, looking at Ireland in isolation, sought some way to appease Irish republican violence. This approach presupposed that the Union had failed, but anyone who looked at Ulster

◀ *An anti-Home Rule demonstration in Ulster*

could see the opposite to be true. There shipbuilding and linen thrived on the basis of a 'great interweaving of interests' and even closer 'business and industrial relations' with England and Scotland.

The following year a Protestant militia, the Ulster Volunteer Force (UVF), was raised to forcibly resist any moves towards self-government in Ireland. It became a force to be reckoned with when a boat-load of arms were landed in Northern Ireland in April 1914. Despite the fierce resistance, a bill granting Home Rule was passed through its parliamentary stages – only to be postponed because of the outbreak of the First World War.

▲ *Volunteers waiting to join the army at the start of the First World War*

Gun-running at Larne

By the end of 1913, the UVF had about 100,000 members, and moves were afoot to arm them properly.

THE GOVERNMENT HAD largely turned a blind eye to their activities, as they were not seen as a threat to the British Empire. As a result, when 24,000 rifles and several million rounds of ammunition were landed at Larne in April 1914, the military authorities did not intervene.

Also at the end of 1913, in an incident which came to be known as the Curragh Mutiny, 58 of the cavalry officers, who were stationed at the British army's headquarters in Ireland, were asked if they would be prepared to take part in actions against the UVF. They all stated that they would prefer to be dismissed than required to wage war on the UVF.

◀ *Polo, often played by English army officers, was seen as a symbol of the British Empire*

THE IRB

At the same time, the Irish Republican Brotherhood (IRB) – the military organisation which had been formed in 1858 in the lead-up to the Fenian insurrection – became active once more. Although the Fenians had been heavily defeated, their teachings had not been forgotten. Some of their supporters were active in the Land League and others got involved in the Gaelic Athletic Association (GAA). The GAA, in fact, proved to be the link between the older Fenians and the younger generation of nationalists.

The IRB came to the fore when the Irish Volunteers were publicly launched at a mass meeting in the Rotunda, Dublin in November 1913. As early as 1907, Thomas J. Clarke, a veteran of the Fenian campaign, had returned from American exile. He had begun to reorganise the IRB, often taking members from Sinn Fein, an ideological and political movement rather than a military one.

A newspaper illustration of a makeshift 'factory' where Fenian members created explosives ▶

The Labour Movement in Ireland

Apart from the UVF and the Irish Volunteers, there was another unofficial army in Ireland.

THE EARLY YEARS of the twentieth century had also seen the rise of a labour movement, concentrated mainly in Dublin where the working classes often lived in dreadful poverty; wages were low and unemployment high.

James Connolly, who had been born in Edinburgh of Irish parents, came to Ireland in 1896 and founded the Irish Socialist Republican Party. For him, the twin issues of workers' rights and Irish freedom were inseparable: 'The cause of labour is the cause of Ireland, the cause of Ireland is the cause of labour. They cannot be dissevered.'

The stated aims of the ISRP were the establishment of an Irish socialist republic based upon the public ownership by the Irish people of the land, and instruments of production, distribution and exchange. Agriculture would be administered as a public function, under boards of management elected by the agricultural population and responsible to them and to the nation at large. All other forms of labour necessary to the well-being of the community would be conducted on the same principles.

▲ *James Connolly*

Just as Connolly was convinced of the necessity of the leadership of the working class, so too he realised that its fate was inseparably involved with that of the peasantry, with whom union must be established if national and social liberation were to be attained. He stood for the Leninist interpretation of this alliance, both in theory and in practice. Since the Irish question, at least until the beginning of the twentieth century, fundamentally revolved around the question, 'who possesses the land and governs?' he took as starting point the understanding of the Irish struggle for freedom.

▲ *'Who possesses the land and governs?'*

The 1913 Strikes and the Formation of the Citizen Army

In 1913, following a baton charge by police on a crowd listening to the other significant Labour leader, James Larkin, the Irish Citizen Army was formed for the purpose of protecting and supporting striking workers and protesters. 1913 was also the year of the Great Transport Strike, or the 'Great Lock-Out', which involved some 24,000 workers in Dublin.

ORGANISED BY JAMES LARKIN and the Irish Transport General Workers' Union, this began as a strike for better wages and conditions among tramwaymen and soon involved other poorly paid workers. These strikes were followed by a lock-out, and a bitter struggle continued for five months, with the employers emerging victorious early in 1914.

James Connolly, who had spent three years organising union activity in Belfast, was recalled to Dublin along with J. R. White, a northern Protestant nationalist who had military experience with the British army. The formation of the Citizen Army just a few weeks before that of the Irish Volunteers was an important stimulus for military activity within nationalism.

The Irish Citizen Army was born out of the struggle between the workers and the employers during the Great Lock-Out. According to William O'Brien's recollections in the book *Forth The Banners Go*, the name of the Citizen Army came from the Social Democratic Federation

James Larkin ▶

who, in the early 1880's, planned to form a citizen army to replace the state army.

Considering the strong working-class character of the Irish Citizen Army, it is surprising that members of the Anglo-Irish aristocracy were involved in its formation. The diversity in the backgrounds of, on the one hand, Countess Constance Markievicz and Jack White and those of James Connolly and Jim Larkin on the other, could not be more pronounced.

Labour Instigates Unrest

The workers of Ireland now felt that they were part of a movement that would see Ireland being controlled by the Irish, and the Labour movement was instrumental in this.

AT ONE OF THE HUGE nightly rallies in Beresford Place, Larkin announced a public meeting to be held the following Sunday, in O'Connell Street, in support of the strikers. In doing so he promised that 'if one of our class fall then two of the other should fall for that one.'

The following day the Irish Transport General Workers' Union leadership – which included Larkin, William O'Brien, P. T. Daly, William Partridge and Thomas Lawlor – were arrested and charged with seditious

libel and conspiracy. All five men were released after giving an undertaking to be of 'good behaviour'.

Neither the Citizen Army nor the Irish Volunteers were making plans for an insurrection at this stage. In July 1914, the Volunteers landed arms at Howth, County Dublin, in an operation similar to, but much smaller than, that of the Ulster Volunteer Force at Larne earlier in the year.

Troops were sent to seize the weapons but failed and were confronted by a jeering crowd as they returned to their barracks. They opened fire and killed three civilians. Such actions strengthened the Volunteers' position and gave John Redmond less room to manoeuvre in parliament.

The same day as the Howth incident, a conference took place at Buckingham Palace, attended by, among others, Sir Edward Carson and James Craig on the unionist side and John Redmond and John Dillon on the nationalist side. They failed to come to any agreement over possible modifications to the Home Rule Bill, which was due to become law in just a few weeks' time.

◄ *Dublin's O'Connell Street, where the meeting was to be held*

▲ *Sir James Craig*

Home Rule Postponed by the First World War

As Europe prepared for war, both sides of the religious divide in Ireland were armed and organised and it seemed inevitable that one side or the other must come into direct conflict with the government. However, events on a larger stage were to defer the crisis when August 1914 saw the outbreak of war between Britain and Germany.

At the end of the war it was to be seen that the ethnic hatred, racism, and nationalism of the post-war period merely planted the seeds of a second terrible conflict. The war solved nothing. The sacrifices were to produce no security and the decisions of the Peace Conference were to produce no peace.

By placing the chief blame for the war on Germany in the famous 'War Guilt Clause', the Allied Powers crippled the new democratic government of Germany and alienated every German patriot. Germany refused to acknowledge their part in bringing on the war, and the Allies refused to accept the terrible consequences their sanctions would impose on an already decimated nation – the Depression that ensued created a smooth pathway to success for Adolf Hitler, his promise of a brighter future and his terrifying 'Final Solution'. In all, the entirety of Europe was affected irrevocably by the First World War, ironically referred to as the 'Great War'. It destroyed a relatively peaceful century of progress, ruined the very dynasties which it was initiated to save, and laid the foundations for other dictators, such as Lenin and Mussolini, as well as Hitler.

A German cartoon of 1914 showing Ireland receiving Home Rule for assistance in the war ▶

Ireland was as much affected by the First World War, as its European neighbours. Both Redmond and Carson put aside their personal differences and agreed to support the war effort meaning that although the Home Rule Bill was to pass into law, at the same time another Act would be passed suspending its implementation until the end of the war. This delay was to change the course of Irish history.

New Armies

The outbreak of the First World War was regarded by Sir Edward Carson as an opportunity for the unionists to demonstrate their loyalty and win sympathy and support from the British government and public. He persuaded the authorities to absorb the UVF into the regular army as the 36th (Ulster) Division.

TOWARDS THE END of 1914, Lord Kitchener – the Minister of War, foresaw that the war would not soon end. Faced with this fact and with so many regular and territorial soldiers already in France, he decided on a new and bold remedy. He would build a 'New Army' composed of civilian volunteers raised from all areas of the British Isles. While it was being trained, the regulars and territorials would hold the enemy in France.

Thus it came about that the New Army of 'Kitchener's Men' was created. By the end of the year, nearly 1,200,000 men had enlisted. As a result, one of the new divisions created was the 36th (Ulster) Division – known to many English Soldiers as 'Carson's Army'.

▲ *The Battle of the Somme, 1916*

This unit was to suffer the loss of 5,500 men in one day – 1 July 1916 – the first day of the Battle of the Somme, a tragedy that had lasting repercussions for unionist Ulster. The people who had paid this terrible price to demonstrate their loyalty to Britain now felt that to deviate in any way from this loyalty would be an insult to the memory of those who gave their lives.

John Redmond had also encouraged the Irish Volunteers to enlist and many did so, believing that their support for the war effort would be rewarded with Home Rule after the war. The National Volunteers, as they became known, were not treated in the same way as the UVF. Instead, they were dispersed throughout the regular army.

▲ *Thousands of Irish volunteers died during the horrors of the war*

Preparing for the Rising

After the start of the Great War, the Supreme Council of the IRB called together the leaders of other progressive parties, and a decision was taken to utilise the opportunity offered by the war to rise in arms against the English.

THOMAS CLARKE was the main instigator of the proposed uprising; in this he was supported by Patrick Pearse, Seán Mac Diarmada, Eamonn Ceant and Seán T. O'Ceallaigh. The latter was sent to America in order to raise further assistance.

New members Thomas McDonagh, Joseph Plunket and James Connolly were later brought on to the Council, while Plunket's sister, Philomena, was sent to New York with a message to be transmitted to Germany. The message with which she was entrusted read 'The arms must

▲ *Germany was eager to ally itself with Ireland*

not be landed before the night of Easter Sunday, 23 April. This vital. Smuggling impossible.'

A large section of the Irish Volunteers rejected Redmond's call to help the war effort. They regrouped under the leadership of Eoin MacNeill who believed it was important for the Irish Volunteers to maintain their strength in Ireland so that there could be no back-tracking on the Home Rule Bill after the war. Others, such as James Connolly and Arthur Griffith, refused to fight because they saw the war as England's war and stated that Ireland had no quarrel with Germany. However there were also Volunteers who were members of the IRB as well. Their view was that 'England's difficulty was Ireland's opportunity'.

In 1915, the IRB formed a military council. Although many of its members were also members of the Irish Volunteers, they kept their leader, Eoin MacNeill, in the dark about their plans for a rising.

James Connolly ▶

Patrick Pearse and the Funeral of O'Donovan Rossa

Dublin-born Patrick H. Pearse (*Padraig Mac Piarais*) (1879–1916) was one of the most prominent figures of this period. Joining the Gaelic League in 1896, he played a significant role in the development of the organisation and in the promotion of its aims, especially in the fields of education and literature in Irish.

PEARSE PUT HIS revolutionary ideas into practice by founding an Irish-medium school and laying the foundations of a new literature in Irish, by writing some of the first modern short stories and poetry in that language.

Like many other uncompromising Irish rebels, Pearse was not of pure Irish blood; instead he was the product of a mixed English-Irish marriage. His father, an Englishman, was a monumental sculpto, his mother was a native of County Meath. Pearse began his life-long study of the Irish language at the age of 11; perhaps his strident nationalism was a by-product of his study of the language which the British had tried so hard to destroy over the last few centuries.

After graduation from the Royal University of Ireland, Pearse was called to the bar, although he never practised. He joined the Gaelic League in 1895 and in 1908, along with friends Thomas MacDonagh, Con Colbert and his brother William, Pearse founded an Irish language school called St Enda's at Cullenwood House in Rathmines, outside Dublin.

Pearse wrote a great deal of prose and poetry, some in Irish and some in English, much of which was published after his death. He also contributed articles to Arthur Griffith's *The United Irishman*. He was becoming more and more radical in his outlook on Irish freedom,

▲ *Bilingual signposts in County Kerry*

▲ *The controversial playwright, John Millington Synge,*
an important part of Ireland's literary heritage

evolving from being a supporter of Home Rule to being a republican. In 1913, he was one of the founders of the Irish Volunteers, a native Irish militia that would later evolve into the Irish Republican Army. Later that year, Pearse joined the Irish Republican Brotherhood and became committed to the use of force to achieve political revolution.

A significant event in 1915 was the funeral of Jeremiah O'Donovan Rossa, in Glasnevin cemetery, on 1 August. The old Fenian had died in America but his body had been repatriated. An armed guard consisting of members of the Citizen Army and the Irish Volunteers flanked the hearse and mourners came from all over the country to be present. Patrick Pearse judged the mood of the country to perfection and the words of his graveside oration have continued to echo down through the years.

'Life springs from death; and from the graves of patriot men and women spring living nations. The defenders of this Realm have worked well in secret and in the open. They think they have pacified Ireland. They think they have purchased half of us and intimidated the other half. They think that they have foreseen everything, they think they have provided against everything; but the fools, the fools, the fools, they have left us our Fenian dead, and while Ireland holds these graves, Ireland unfree shall never be at peace.'

Pearse was elected president of the provisional government of the Irish Republic of 1916 and created commandant-general of its forces during the rising. Condemned to death in a subsequent British court-martial, he was executed by firing squad on 3 May 1916.

▲ *British attempts to subdue the Irish language were unsuccessful*

The Rising is Postponed

The rebellion was organised by the IRB and not Sinn Fein. They had financial help from America. James Connolly was party to developments and promised the support of the Citizen Army, which numbered about 200.

I N THE WEEKS leading up to the planned rising at Easter 1916, the Irish Volunteers and the Citizen Army held a series of parades, hoping that when the time came for them to take action they would be able to catch the authorities off their guard. The IRB hoped to have 10,000 in action on the appointed day. Several things happened immediately prior to this that were to blunt the military effect of the rising.

The rising was due to take place on Easter Sunday, 23 April 1916, but on the Thursday previous Eoin MacNeill found out about it and, believing that the Irish Volunteers would be hopelessly outnumbered and inadequately armed, gave orders cancelling all manoeuvres.

The following day, however, word came through of a German ship, the *Aud*, bringing arms and ammunition. Then the next day (Saturday), the ship was captured and scuttled by her crew. Sir Roger Casement, who had been in Germany organising support, was arrested in County Kerry after landing there by U-boat. MacNeill, believing that there was no hope

▲ *James Connolly was executed after the 1916 rising*

of success, once more issued orders cancelling all Volunteer activities planned for the following day.

The rising was ill conceived. As there weren't enough Volunteers to carry all the guns, some had to be abandoned or hidden for further collection. Word reached the Citizen Army at Croydon Park of the days happenings and some members went to see if they could be of assistance.

▲ *James Casement trying to persuade Irish soldiers to defect*

On arriving in the area they were delighted to find abandoned and hidden arms, which they brought back to Croydon Park for use by the Citizen Army.

Rifles were also smuggled into Dublin through Liverpool, sent by supportive trade unionists in Britain. Another avenue for the procurement of arms was through British soldiers, either stolen by supportive soldiers or sold by entrepreneurial members of her Majesty's Armed Services.

James Connolly had been using the pages of the I. T. G. W. U.'s *Irish Worker* to argue against working-class participation in the imperialist war. He urged people to join the Volunteers or the Citizen Army rather than the British army. He was a great believer in the old maxim that England's difficulty was Ireland's opportunity and, with England involved in a war, now was the time for Ireland to assert itself.

ROGER CASEMENT

A REPUBLICAN FROM a north Antrim Protestant family, Sir Roger Casement (1864–1916) had been knighted in 1911 for his humanitarian work in exposing the brutal cruelties of the colonial regime in the Belgian Congo where he had been based as a British diplomat. Returning home, he became involved in the Gaelic League in Ulster and, in 1913, he was appointed treasurer of the Irish Volunteers. One of the organisers of the Howth gun-running operation, he later travelled to Germany to procure more arms and to recruit among Irish prisoners-of-war held there. The Germans, however, were only prepared to send arms. Casement rushed back to Ireland, where he was arrested. He was hanged for treason after a trial in London.

A German cartoon of 1914 showing Germany offering Ireland Home Rule in return for assistance in the war ▶

The Rising Takes Place

Pearse, Connolly and the other IRB leaders were determined to press ahead, and sent word to their supporters that the rising would begin on Easter Monday – a Bank Holiday – when the city would be quiet.

THE DAY WAS fine and sunny. Dublin was in a relaxed mood as people strolled about enjoying the sunshine. Many had gone to the races at Fairyhouse. Few people paid any attention as hundreds of Volunteers and Citizen Army men assembled at Liberty Hall and then marched away to various points about the city. They were too used to route marches and mock battles to expect that this morning would be any different.

This time, however, the Volunteers were in earnest. About noon they seized a series of strongpoints around the centre of the city and began to fortify them against attack. In O'Connell Street, the General Post Office was occupied and, while his men sand-bagged the windows behind him, Pearse, pale and tense, came to the steps and read to a puzzled and indifferent crowd, the Proclamation of the Provisional Government of the Irish Republic. The signatories were Thomas J. Clarke, Sean Mac Diarmada, Thomas MacDonagh, P. H. Pearse, Eamonn Ceannt, James Connolly and Joseph Plunkett.

However, they failed to take Dublin Castle and the telephone exchange and, once the authorities realised that this was intended as something more significant than a protest or a show of strength, they were able to summon reinforcements.

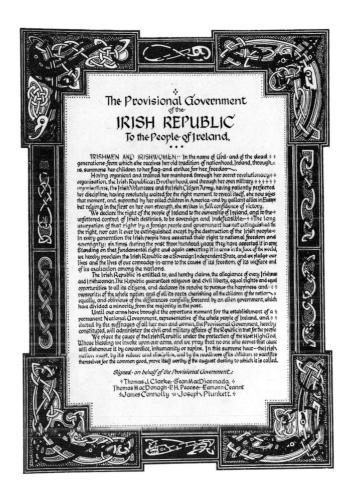

▲ The 1916 Declaration of Independence

The Progress of the Rising

As the reinforcements began to arrive on Tuesday and artillery was brought into play, the fighting intensified. About 2,000 people had taken part in the rising, but now they were trapped in the positions they had captured as the country in general, and the people of Dublin in particular, had failed to respond to their call. There was no likelihood of reinforcements for the rebels and their positions appeared increasingly isolated.

BRITISH ARTILLERY PLAYED a key role and there was nothing that the rebels with their rifles could do about it. A British gun-boat, the *Helga*, came up the River Liffey into the city centre and proceeded to shell O'Connell Street and the GPO.

*Irish Rebellion, May 1916
Soldiers holding a Dublin Street.*

Once the rebels had occupied some of their targeted buildings, they had nowhere to go. The rest of Ireland showed little inclination to join the rising, apart from a few minor outbreaks of violence, and in Dublin there were few recruits. The government, which had not expected a rising, responded quickly by declaring martial law. The army in Dublin was reinforced, and heavy artillery was deployed against the republican strongholds. On the Friday, General Sir John Maxwell arrived from England to assume overall

▲ *Government troops barricading a street during the uprising* command, and made it clear that he would not hesitate to destroy every building held by the rebels. The GPO – headquarters of the rebels – was soon in flames.

In different circumstances, the rebels might have been treated more mercifully, but Britain was at war, and the army and police had suffered greater casualties than Pearse's men. Ireland was still under martial law, and Maxwell was at liberty to inflict retribution.

The cover of Irish Life *after the Easter Rebellion* ▶

The Ignominious End

The rising had lasted less than a week and it appeared, from a military point of view, to have been a complete failure.

THERE HAD BEEN many casualties, especially among the rebels and civilians, along with serious damage to property in central Dublin. During the rising, British gunboats in the Liffey bombarded Dublin's city centre.

The thought of an occupying navy sailing into the centre of a city and laying waste to its civilians and buildings was too much for many to bear. Over 500 persons lost their lives in the fighting, the majority of them non-combatant civilians. Volunteer activities in other parts of the country had been isolated and rendered insignificant.

The official surrender document, signed by both parties, stated: 'In order to prevent the further slaughter of Dublin and in the hope of

▲ *Dublin's main Post Office, gutted by fire during the Easter Rising* saving the lives of our followers, now surrounded and hopelessly outnumbered, the members of the Provisional Government present at Head-Quarters have agreed to an unconditional surrender and the Commandants of the various districts in the City and Country will order their commands to lay down arms.'

It was signed by 'P. H. Pearse' at 3.45 p.m. on 29 April 1916.

This historic document was then followed by two handwritten statements, the first by James Connolly – 'I agree to these conditions for the men only under my own command in the Moore Street district and for the men in the Stephen's Green Command.' – and then by Thomas MacDonagh – 'On consultation with Commandant Ceannt and other officers I have decided to agree to unconditional surrender also'.

▼ *Dublin's rebuilt Post Office houses a sculpture dedicated to those who died in the Civil War*

Executions of the Leaders

Martial law was imposed and in a series of court-martials between 3 and 12 May, 15 leaders of the insurrection, including the seven signatories of the Proclamation were found guilty and executed by firing squad. James Connolly, who had been wounded, was executed tied to a chair.

FINALLY THE executions were halted – as the British government responded to a wave of public revulsion – but the damage had already been done. Ireland had new martyrs, and earlier apathy, or even hostility, towards republicanism was replaced by sympathy for their independence cause. Of some 3,400 arrested following the surrender, more than half were imprisoned or interned in England, while many others were sent to Frongoch in Wales. From these prison camps, they plotted a new onslaught on British rule.

Up to this point, as is obvious from the freedom to march and drill previously given to the Irish Volunteers and the Citizen Army, the British

▲ *Police and British soldiers surround a farm occupied by Sinn Fein*

▲ *Captured Sinn Fein rebels being escorted through Dublin*

Government had been adopting a very low-key approach to the maintenance of law and order in Ireland. The war on the continent had released the pressure that had been building up over the question of Home Rule and there had appeared to be little significant threat.

Many of the men executed and imprisoned were well-known national figures because of their involvement in groups such as the Volunteers and the Gaelic League. Several were known as writers or poets; their deaths caused great anger and resentment. As each passing day brought the announcement of further executions, the mood in the country changed quickly.

The sixteenth person to be executed for his part in the rising was Sir Roger Casement. After being tried as a traitor, he was hanged in London, on 3 August 1916.

Eamon de Valera and Countess Markievicz

Of the leaders who avoided execution, the most significant were Eamon de Valera, whose death sentence was commuted to life imprisonment so as not to arouse anger in America where he had been born, and Countess Markievicz, who was spared because she was a woman.

THE COUNTESS WAS born into an Anglo-Irish ascendancy family, the Gore-Booths of Sligo. She married a Polish count in 1900, whom she met while studying painting in Paris. A member of the Gaelic League and the Labour movement, she ran a soup kitchen in Dublin for the strikers in 1913. She was an officer in the Citizen Army, a republican and a feminist. She was the first woman elected as a Westminster MP though she did not take her seat, in line with Sinn Fein policy. She later joined De Valera's Fianna Fail party.

De Valera was released from prison in June 1917, along with others who had been sentenced to terms of imprisonment. This towering personality in Irish politics for most of the twentieth century was born in

▲ *De Valera (second from right), photographed with the Irish political delegates, in 1922*

New York in 1882, to an Irish mother and Spanish father. His father died when Eamon was two years old and he was sent to his mother's family in County Limerick. The circumstances of his birth were to ensure his survival – the British authorities decided that executing him along with the other leaders of the Easter Rising would antagonise people in the USA.

Those who had been interned had been released the previous Christmas in an attempt by Lloyd George, now British prime minister, to influence the discussions he was holding between Redmond and Carson. These discussions, however, were largely irrelevant, since Sinn Fein was not involved.

▼ *De Valera and Lloyd George meet at Downing Street in 1921*

Bi-election Victories for Sinn Fein

Until the late summer of 1917, Sinn Fein was little more than a loosely organised collection of local clubs scattered throughout the country.

MOVES WERE THEN BEGUN to bring them under some sort of central co-ordinating control and to hammer out a comprehensive set of policy objectives acceptable to all. The *ard-fheis*, or conference, was held on 25 October 1917.

Thanks to the ingenuity of de Valera, a formula of Sinn Fein's basic principles had been devised which would reconcile the republican and non-republican sections of the movement: Sinn Fein aimed at securing the international recognition of Ireland as an independent Irish Republic. Having achieved that status, the Irish people would, by referendum, freely choose their own form of Government.

Since the rising, the mood in the country had changed to such an extent that, politically,

◄ *Eamon de Valera revised Sinn Fein's policies in 1917*

Redmond and his party were now a spent force, something which would soon become apparent. The months spent in captivity had given the surviving leaders of the IRB ample opportunity to formulate new plans. The Volunteers were reorganised and Sinn Fein came to the fore as the political wing of the republican movement. In Roscommon in February and in Longford in May 1917, Sinn Fein won bi-elections on an abstentionist ticket. These seats had previously been comfortably held by Redmondites.

In July 1917, De Valera was elected MP for East Clare. He took over the leadership of Sinn Fein from Arthur Griffith in October. In November was also made president of the Irish Volunteers.

▲ *De Valera inspecting troops of the Irish Republican Army*

The Rise Of Michael Collins

Michael Collins, who had been *aide-de-camp* to Joseph Plunkett – one of the executed signatories of the 1916 proclamation – and who had, himself, been interned after the rising, also came to prominence at this time.

COLLINS WAS GIVEN the title of Director of Organisations for the Volunteers. A straight-forward, no-nonsense man, he understood what was required to wage a guerrilla war against the British and was not afraid to act accordingly.

By attempting to introduce conscription early in 1918, the British government managed to anger, and unite, all shades of nationalist opinion in Ireland. The Home Rule Party MPs withdrew their presence from Westminster and a successful national one-day strike was called.

The British government then decided to take a firm line with the anti-conscription agitation and sent Field-Marshal Lord French to Ireland, as the new Lord Lieutenant with powers of coercion. French was a

◀ *General Michael Collins (left) on parade*

tough-minded military man and it was widely believed that he had come to Ireland to enforce conscription.

A week after his arrival, French swooped down on the anti-conscriptionists. On the night of 17 May the leaders of Sinn Fein, the Volunteers, the Gaelic League and several other nationalist organisations were arrested. Collins and Brugha were the only prominent nationalists to evade the net. Griffith and De Valera were arrested. Two months later all the leading nationalist organisations were suppressed.

The end of the First World War in November 1918 was followed by a general election in December. This saw 73 Sinn Fein, 26 Unionist and 6 Irish Party MPs returned. Now, rather than take their seats at Westminster, the Sinn Fein MPs met in Dublin in January 1919. They formed *Dail Eireann* – Ireland's Assembly – the name still given to the Irish parliament. Not all Sinn Fein's MPs were present; 34 were in gaol and one had been deported.

▼ *After the 1919 General Election, Ireland's parliament met in Ireland, not Westminster*

The First Dail

After his dramatic escape from Lincoln gaol in early 1919, De Valera was elected President of the Dail. He and his appointed ministers then claimed authority as the elected Irish government, an authority which came to be accepted throughout most of the country as the months progressed

THE FIRST SESSION of Dail Eireann (Assembly of Ireland) was held in the Mansion House, Dublin on 21 January 1919. Invitations had been sent to all the Irish MPs elected in 1918, but unionists and the surviving Home Rulers refused to participate, the attendance therefore being limited to the Sinn Fein members. Since many of these were in prison or absent for other reasons, no more than 27 were present.

▲ *Irish MPs photographed in 1922*

The session lasted for only two hours, and most of its proceedings were in Irish. Cathal Brugha acted as provisional president of the Assembly. At this meeting several documents were read and approved: a provisional constitution; a declaration of independence; a 'Message to the Free Nations of the World'; and a socio-economic policy document known as the 'Democratic Programme'.

The adoption of the provisional constitution marks the beginning of the present 26–county state. The Dail's main concern was the setting up of the necessary machinery for running an independent Irish government. It adopted the same kind of parliamentary procedure and the same kind of civil service as existed in England.

The Dail formally ratified the republic which had been proclaimed in 1916 and selected delegates to the post-war Peace Conference at Paris. It was hoped that the Irish Republic would secure recognition from the other European powers at this conference.

▲ *British prime minister, Lloyd George, photographed in 1916*

The War Of Independence

The War of Independence can be said to have started on the day the first Dail convened, 21 January 1919, with an attack on an explosives convoy in County Tipperary. In the attack, two constables were shot dead and the explosives seized.

THE IRISH VOLUNTEERS, renamed the Irish Republican Army (IRA) in 1919, began operating as a guerrilla force, attacking both the police and the military. Many of these attacks, especially in the early months of the campaign, were launched with the specific aim of obtaining arms and ammunition.

Even in the early stages, the British government appeared to lack a coherent policy towards Ireland, other than one of partial containment. The situation gradually deteriorated as the republicans expanded and strengthened their military forces. Especially useful was help from the United States, where De Valera was a frequent visitor in 1919 and 1920.

The war in Ireland was costing the British taxpayers £20 million a year. Prime minister Lloyd George was gradually forced to admit to himself that he was fighting not a massive crime wave but a popular organised movement for national liberation, operating by means of a guerrilla army. Once he had conceded this point, only two courses of action were open to him: he must either inflict a total military defeat on the guerrilla forces, or he must negotiate with the enemy.

Lloyd George was also aware that the influential USA President Wilson, who despite his loathing for Irish-American nationalists and his

Map showing the boundaries between Northern Ireland and the Republic of Ireland ▶

persistent refusal to recognise the Irish Republic, was anxious that the British government should effect a speedy and just settlement of the Irish question. Thus the second alternative was the only practicable one. In Ireland, too, there was a growing desire for peace.

NORTHERN IRELAND

REPUBLIC OF IRELAND

The Government of Ireland Act

The IRA, having fought for two years against heavy odds, had suffered severe losses, both of men and equipment, and were in a shaky condition. Michael Collins later admitted that at the time of the truce they could not have held out for another three weeks.

L OYD GEORGE'S earliest attempts to promote a peace initiative failed, mainly because he was unwilling to recognise the IRA's belligerent status, and insisted that they must surrender unconditionally before discussion could begin. This, of course, was something they refused to do.

He also totally rejected the idea of negotiating with Michael Collins, whom Lloyd George believed, at this stage, to be nothing more than a murderous gangster. However, Eamon de Valera, after his return from America at the very end of 1920, was a far more acceptable prospect to the British government. They saw him as an accredited politician who was able to talk the language of diplomacy and who was generally held to be one of the more moderate members of Sinn Fein.

The truce was a moral victory for the movement, since de Valera had relinquished none of his political principles and had won the right for his own government to negotiate directly with the British government. It was a solid and material victory for Irish and British public opinion.

The British government passed the Government of Ireland Act in December 1920. This new Home Rule Bill allowed for the setting up of

Michael Collins, with whom Lloyd George refused to negotiate ▶

parliaments in Dublin and Belfast with powers very similar to those envisaged under the 1914 Act.

The new province to be known as 'Northern Ireland' was to consist of six counties – County Derry, County Antrim, County Down, County Armagh, County Fermanagh and County Tyrone; 'Southern Ireland' was to be made up of the remaining 26. To the republicans, the very idea of proposing a measure of Home Rule at this stage was perceived as an insult and an irrelevance.

However, they used the subsequent election as a show of strength, winning, unopposed, 124 of the 128 seats in 'Southern Ireland'. As members of Sinn Fein, they then ignored the new parliament and used

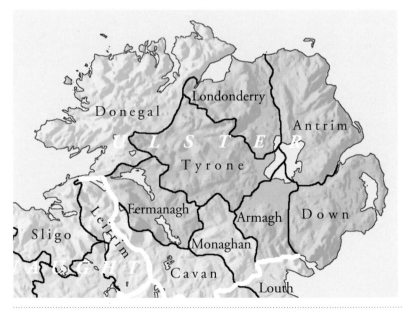

▲ *The counties of Northern Ireland*

this mandate to form the second Dail. The political entity known as 'Southern Ireland' had been still-born.

The partition of Ireland as arranged under this legislation had been prefigured in the arguments that had raged in the British parliament prior to the passing of the 1912 Home Rule act. Carson had proposed the exclusion of the nine counties of Ulster in the hope that such an amendment would make Home Rule so unpalatable for nationalists as to invalidate the Bill altogether in their eyes.

▲ *Sir James Craig, the new prime minister of Ireland*

The Black and Tans and State Security

The first of a new generation of English police recruits arrived in Ireland in March 1920. They were not the type of men who would have been accepted by any police force in normal circumstances. They were young men who had served in the war and had been unable to find work after their demobilisation.

IN THE POST-WAR economic depression that had struck Britain, unemployment was at a very high level. Few employers were prepared to offer steady jobs to untrained men whose wartime experiences had given them a taste for adventure and had hardened them to violence and brutality. Such men eagerly grasped the opportunity to return to the only kind of life they knew or cared about – and at the very attractive wage of 10 shillings a day.

On their arrival in Ireland, it was found that there were not enough of the dark police uniforms to go round, and the missing items of clothing were supplied from khaki army uniforms. Their part-coloured outfits inspired the nickname 'Black and Tans' and also served to symbolise their anomalous position: they were technically policemen but they acted as a military combat force.

A second armed force, the Auxiliaries, was created in August 1920 to supplement the Black and Tans. The Auxiliaries were ex-officers and tended to be slightly older, tougher and more responsible than the Black and Tans. They formed an élite commando-style force. They were paid £1 a day and were allowed considerable freedom of action.

David Lloyd George ▶

As well as sending the police reinforcements to Ireland, Lloyd George made a number of changes at a higher administrative level. He appointed a new chief secretary, Sir Hamar Greenwood, who adopted the policy of allowing the forces of law and order a free hand in their struggle against terrorism.

The Original Bloody Sunday

In the second half of 1920, there were about 30,000 regular soldiers in Ireland, as well as 11,000 police (including the Black and Tans and Auxiliaries).

HE SOLDIERS REMAINED to some extent outside the struggle, partly because the IRA was reluctant to pit its strength against experienced professional soldiers, and partly because Lloyd George did not want the army to play an active role in maintaining peace.

The Black and Tans quickly found that fighting the IRA was a very different matter to fighting the Germans. The First World War had been conducted according to the international rules of war. The opposing armies were very clearly recognisable to one another; they were ranged in trenches that faced each other across a clearly defined no man's land; they advanced

▲ *Armies could see each other in the First World war, while fighting the IRA was like guerrilla warfa*

or retreated across definite tracts of territory and measured their progress by the amount of land they could defend behind their front line.

In the kind of guerrilla warfare that now prevailed in Ireland there were no rules; there was no front line, or rather the front line was everywhere; the enemy was invisible – but he was everywhere. The IRA wore no uniform (since this would have immediately invited the attention of the numerous superior British forces), and an apparently innocent group of by-standers could suddenly be transformed into a detachment of armed men who could strafe an RIC patrol with gunfire and then slip away quickly and quietly to mingle with the local population.

▼ *Civil War in Ireland: a bomb in a Dublin park*

In conditions like these, the Black and Tans' nerves were strained to breaking-point. Their pent-up tensions sometimes exploded in deeds of inhuman savagery. It was quite possible for a harmless man to be shot simply for having his hands in his pockets. Ordinary people throughout the country felt that they were being terrorised by the Black and Tans. Whereas the independently operating Volunteers of 1918–19 had been regarded by many people as something of a nuisance, by the end of 1920 they were seen as the only defenders of public safety against the British forces.

▲ *Troops with a Lewis gun, guarding a street corner*

The 1920s was a decade of bloodshed in Ireland. The Black and Tans' frustration was to explode in what became known as 'Bloody Sunday', one of the worst single events of the era. It would become an emotional symbol of the horror of the times.

As the summer of 1920 drew to a close, the death toll from the conflict rose steadily. On 21 November 1920, IRA leader Michael Collins ordered the death in Dublin of 11 men he believed were spies for the British. The IRA carried out his orders and killed another three British soldiers in the process, bringing the toll of those killed by the group to 14.

British 'Black and Tans' took revenge that same afternoon. They drove their armoured cars into a Dublin stadium, where a large crowd was watching a Gaelic football game, and turned their guns on the fans. Thirteen Irish people were killed and scores were wounded. Bloody Sunday finally drew to a close with two suspected IRA members being killed by their captors in Dublin Castle.

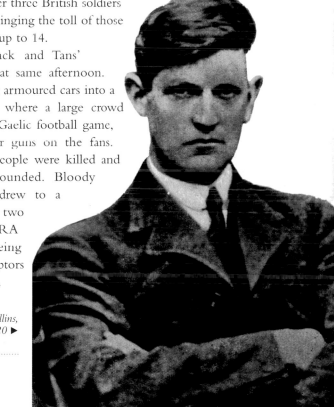

Michael Collins, photographed in 1920 ▶

The Irish Take a Stand

The British Government hoped that the use of such force would break not only the IRA but also the will of the civilian population. They reckoned that, by creating so much havoc and terror, the Irish people would turn their backs on the IRA, and yearn for peace.

THE IRA, being a plain-clothes guerrilla army was difficult to engage, and Sir Hamar Greenwood, the chief secretary appointed in mid-1920, believed that the police and military should be able to take the law into their own hands and fight terror with terror. A policy of reprisals by government forces, which initially had merely been condoned, soon became officially authorised and, by the beginning of 1921, some of the most notorious incidents of the IRA–British government war had already taken place.

▲ *US submarines bringing arms to Sinn Fein*

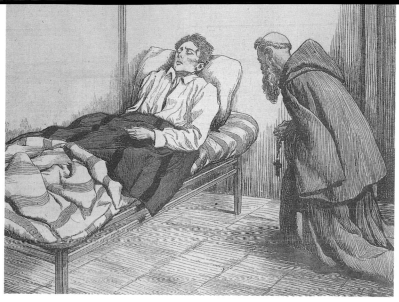

▲ *Terence MacSwiney, nearing the end of his fatal hunger strike*

In March 1920, Tomas MacCurtain, Lord Mayor of Cork City, had been shot dead in his own home by Royal Irish Constabulary men posing as civilians. His successor, Terence MacSwiney, who was arrested on a charge of having in his possession 'documents likely to cause disaffection to his Majesty', died in Brixton prison after a hunger strike of 74 days.

An earlier hunger striker was Thomas Ashe, a Sinn Fein member arrested in 1917; Ashe had died after the prison authorities had attempted to force-feed him. His funeral, which was organised by Michael Collins, was attended by 9,000 Irish Volunteers and 30,000 other mourners. Terence MacSwiney's funeral in Cork was also a deeply moving and politically significant occasion. Irish history would show that the hunger strike, though painful and emotional for all concerned, would become a useful weapon in focusing friends and foes alike.

The Burning of Cork

Cork has been home to many great men, such as the young William Penn, who lived in Cork in the late seventeenth century, as the attaché of the vice regal court in Ireland. In the nineteenth century, Henry Ford emigrated from Ballinascarty on the Clonakilty-to-Bandon Road. In 1917, the Ford Company established in Cork their first factory outside the United States.

CORK WAS ALSO John Redmond and Michael Collins country. Initially, Cork had received the name 'rebel' when Perkin Warbeck, a pretender to the British throne, came to Ireland seeking support for his cause. He found it in the 'establishment' in Cork, mainly in the figure of Mayor John Walters. When Warbeck was executed for his treason, Walters met the same fate, and Cork had its charter withdrawn – Cork has always been republican by nature.

◄ *Henry Ford, whose first non-US factory was opened in Cork*

In December 1920, as a reprisal for several IRA attacks in County Cork, the Black and Tans set fire to the centre of Cork city, destroying the whole of Patrick Street, the City Hall, the library and other public buildings, as well as many shops and businesses. They also obstructed the fire brigade as they tried to tackle the inferno.

Events such as these only served to increase the tension between the sides and to make the Irish more determined than ever to consolidate their independence and get the British forces out of their country once and for all. There could be no going back to the situation that pertained before the First World War. That, however, was the solution proposed by the British government, which passed the Government of Ireland Act in December 1920.

▲ *The River Lee in Cork*

Partition

The Irish Volunteers slowly, almost imperceptibly, began a campaign of violence against those they believed to be agents of the Crown. The violence escalated to frightening proportions. The response of the Black and Tans was as violent as the Volunteers and the killings spiralled out of control.

B Y 1920, THE BRITISH had had enough. Lloyd George's government passed the Better Government for Ireland Act. In 1921, de Valera and Lloyd George met in an effort to hammer a settlement. Lloyd George made it very clear that partition and military concessions were not negotiable. De Valera rejected Lloyd George's terms, but reported them back to the Dail. Both sides agreed to continue the talks. By this stage, the Irish were acutely aware that they had the British on the run, but were also conscious of the fact that they would have to play a smart game to get what they wanted. De Valera, in particular, was not prepared to get drawn in to British games.

Probably in an effort to distance himself from what he viewed as a doomed mission, de Valera did not go himself, but had a four-man commission appointed to continue the talks. Eventually, the commission accepted Lloyd George's terms as probably the best that they could hope for.

The treaty split the Sinn Fein movement: de Valera and his followers walked out of the Dail in protest of its ratification. The split soon hardened in to a full-blown civil war. Both sides had learned well from their experience with the British and the violence that followed was a brutal as anything seen before.

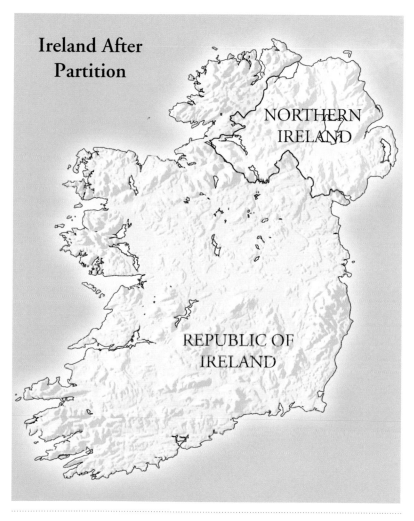

Ireland After
Partition

NORTHERN
IRELAND

REPUBLIC OF
IRELAND

▲ *The Partition of Ireland*

The 1921 Treaty

The Treaty, which was signed on 6 December 1921, agreed that Ireland should become a self-governing dominion within the empire known as the Irish Free State, with the same constitutional status as Canada.

THE BRITISH WERE allowed to retain three naval bases and would be responsible for coastal defence. Northern Ireland was permitted, if its parliament so desired (as everyone knew it did), to opt out of this arrangement and retain the status it had gained under the Government of Ireland Act. Were this to happen, a Boundary Commission was to be set up to determine the exact position of the border.

A lengthy debate ensued in the Dail, culminating in a vote taken on 7 January 1922 accepting the Treaty by 64 to 57. Eamon de Valera, who had voted against it, resigned as President of the Dail and was replaced by Arthur Griffith. Ireland would merely have dominion status within the British Empire and therefore could not be said to be a fully-fledged independent nation.

▲ *Eamon de Valera (photographed in 1958)*

Within a month of the vote, the last viceroy had formally handed over power, along with Dublin Castle – so long the seat of British rule in Ireland – to the provisional government and British troops began to withdraw, handing over their barracks and surplus equipment to the IRA, now regarded as the army of the Irish government.

The nation's first constitution went into effect in 1922, when its name was changed to the Irish Free State. Many felt that it was not an ideal situation or resolution to hundreds of years of conflict with the British. They wanted all or nothing, and would not sit idly by while part of the country was still under British control.

◀ *Signing the 1921 treaty*

Civil War

De Valera regrouped his supporters in a new republican party which would later become known as Fianna Fail. In June 1922, he took on the government in a general election.

THE RESULT WAS a good one for the government, with de Valera's party winning only 35 of 128 seats. The government had taken 58 seats. This vote, taken along with the successes of smaller parties and independents who were not opposed to the treaty, was viewed by them as a vindication of their position. With this mandate, the government hardened its attitude towards the republicans.

Within a fortnight of the general election, hostilities had broken out between the two sides. The republican garrison in the Four Courts building in Dublin kidnapped a government general and, after an ultimatum, Michael Collins ordered the government troops to attack with artillery. The civil war, once begun, became increasingly ugly and traumatic. Both sides had

A two-day battle between Sinn Fein and government troops, 1922 ▶

learned the skills of guerrilla warfare, from their fights against the British, and were well armed.

Anti-Treaty reinforcements had been called from Wicklow, Kildare and Tipperary and they were to mobilise in Blessington, County Wicklow, before marching to Dublin. Earnan O'Maille and Sean Lemass took charge in Blessington and by 1 July the anti-Treaty troops had taken up defensive positions. Meanwhile provisional government troops had begun to push southwards through the Dublin mountains clearing the way as they advanced towards Blessington. These government troops were well-equipped with armoured cars and infantry support and after some exchanges and loss of life, the anti-Treatyites fell back.

The war itself lasted less than a year, but it left a legacy of bitterness and division that was to remain with the country for many years.

▲ *Rebels in Dublin are forced, by fire, to surrender*

The Deaths of Childers, Collins and Griffith

Among the many casualties on both sides were Michael Collins, who died in disputed circumstances aged 32, in an ambush in County Cork, and Erskine Childers, one of those who had been involved in the treaty negotiations in London and who was one of nearly 80 republican prisoners who were executed by the Free State government during the course of the war.

O N 22 AUGUST 1922, on a military tour of West Cork, Michael Collins's convoy was ambushed by anti-Treaty forces at Béal nam Bláth, situated between the towns of Bandon and Macroom. With him in the convoy was General Emmet Dalton, who had taken Cork city by a sea landing. During the exchange of shots between the two forces, Collins was hit by a single shot in the head and was killed. At the age of 31, The 'Big Fellow', as he was known, died only a few miles from his birthplace in his native County Cork. His death sent shock waves around the whole of Ireland. Collins's body

◀ *Erskine Childers*

was taken by sea to Dublin where a state funeral was held.

Arthur Griffith died of a brain haemorrhage in August 1922, aged 50, just 10 days before Collins. William T. Cosgrave succeeded Griffith as president of Dail Eireann and Collins's place was taken by Kevin O'Higgins.

It is interesting to note that Erskine Childers' son, also Erskine Childers, would become fourth president of the Irish Republic in 1974, and that William Cosgrave's son, Liam, would become Taoiseach (prime minister) the same year.

▼ *The death of Michael Collins*

De Valera Forms Fianna Fail

De Valera declared a cease-fire in May 1923, when he realised that victory for his side was impossible.

HIS REPUBLICAN PARTY became Fianna Fail in 1926, but did not take its seats in the Dail until the following year. Five years later, in 1932, de Valera and his party won the general election and formed the new government.

This amazing turn-around in his fortunes was due in part to public disillusionment with the partition element of the treaty. No change in the territory of Northern Ireland had come about as a result of the deliberations of the Boundary Commission.

Economic conditions also played a part as the world economy slumped following the Wall Street Crash, in 1929, and a fall in the exports of foodstuffs hit small farmers especially hard. This was a significant victory, not only for De Valera and his party, but also for democracy in the new state, for it proved that those who could not win using military means could win power through the ballot box.

De Valera's government was determined to pursue its republican agenda, and to remove the oath of allegiance to the British monarch from the Free State constitution and to promote native industries. It also decided to withhold land annuities which were currently paid to the British government.

These were the repayments of loans which had been given under the various land acts to the small farmers to help them buy out their holdings

1923 election posters ▶

from the landlords under the Wyndham Land Act of 1903, and they amounted to some £5 million a year. Britain retaliated by taxing Irish cattle exports and the Free State then responded by adding extra duty to incoming British goods.

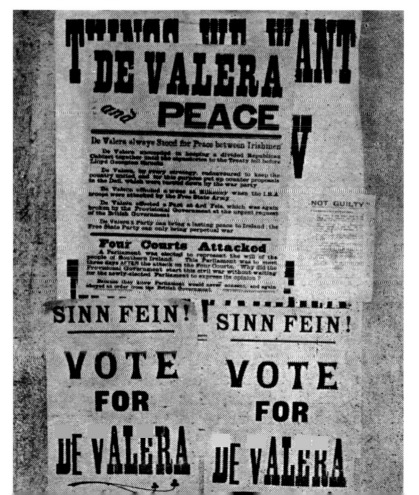

Between the Wars

Throughout the period from the end of the Civil War to the beginning of the Second World War, there had been incidents that threatened to undermine the stability of the state.

I N 1924, THERE had been the threat of an army mutiny, which the government successfully faced down.

Three years later, in July 1927, trouble flared up again with the murder of Kevin O'Higgins. O'Higgins, who was assassinated as he walked to Sunday Mass, had been Cosgrave's deputy; he had also held such important and influential ministries as Home Affairs, External Affairs and Justice.

The emergence of a breakaway republican group caused Cosgrave's government to introduce a tough new Public Safety Bill. This proved unpopular and was probably instrumental in his government's defeat in the 1932 general election.

▲ *The end of the Civil War did not see an end to the fighting*

In power, De Valera found that he, too, had to move against his former colleagues in the IRA, declaring it an illegal organisation in 1936 and again after the outbreak of the Second World War, when many were interned and nine executed. He also sacked Eoin O'Duffy, head of the police force and leader of the fascist group known as the Blueshirts, which had clashed with the IRA on a number of occasions during the 1930s.

In general, however, the early governments of the Irish Free State did a good job in restoring law and order after the years of upheaval and conflict. An unarmed police force, the *Garda Siochana*, was established, while the army was reduced to peacetime levels and restructured.

▲ *De Valera (third from left, front row) with his cabinet*

Ireland on its Own

After the civil war, large parts of the Irish Free State's infrastructure was in turmoil. One of the first tasks was to reconstruct the bridges and railways that had been damaged or destroyed during the war.

OTHER TASKS WHICH were dealt with were: to abolish both the British and the Sinn Fein legal systems and replace them with a new judicial system; to create a civil service; to set up local government and services; to abolish the old workhouses; to reduce the numbers of the swollen army and set up a *gardai* (police); to make

▲ *The new reforms aimed to alleviate the hard lives of poor farming and fishing communities*

education compulsory and introduce Irish language lessons to all schools; to help the poor farmers who made up 70 per cent of the country's population; and to set up an industrial base.

The government also announced freedom of religion for all citizens and a new flag was created, and adopted, for the country to reflect this. The three vertical bands of colour were orange, to represent Protestants; green, to represent Catholics; and white, to represent a state of peace between them. In 1926, Radio Eireann was set up and in 1929 the Shannon Scheme was completed; this harnessed the hydroelectric potential of the River Shannon to supply the new country with much-needed electricity.

So, new structures were developed to replace the British administration and significant economic projects, brought significant financial and social benefits to the country, modernising and updating both urban and rural areas. As the infrastructure, which had been battered by years of fighting, was repaired and replaced, the country developed a new identity and gained status internationally.

▲ *The new flag*

The 1937 Constitution

De Valera introduced a new constitution, *Bunreacht na hEireann*, in 1937, declaring Ireland a 'sovereign, independent, democratic state'. This is the constitution which is still in use today, with several amendments.

THE CONSTITUTION states: 'There shall be a President of Ireland (*Uachtarán na hÉireann*), hereinafter called the President, who shall take precedence over all other persons in the State and who shall exercise and perform the powers and functions conferred on the President by this Constitution and by law.'

The following year, Dr. Douglas Hyde, one of the founders of the Gaelic League in 1893, was elected as Ireland's first President.

Dr Douglas Hyde ▶

THE RETURN OF TREATY PORTS

IN 1938, THE ECONOMIC war with Britain was resolved, with the Irish government paying the British approximately one tenth of what was outstanding in land annuities and in return the British gave up the three ports of Lough Swilly, Berehaven and Cobh, which they had retained under the 1921 treaty. This proved to be an astute move as it enabled the country to remain neutral during the war of 1939–45.

All three were seen as being previously crucial to the defence of the realm. England was acutely aware that Ireland could be a staging post on any attack on Britain, and wished to maintain a force there.

Cobh (pronounced Cove), for instance, is situated on the southern shore of the Great Island in one of the world's finest natural harbours. The town began to develop significantly during the eighteenth century when the harbour became an assembly point for fleets sailing during the Napoleonic Wars. By 1830, Cobh had become a noted health resort and 'watering place', ideal for the typical Victorian holiday. To mark the visit of Queen Victoria in 1849, Cobh was renamed Queenstown and remained such until 1920.

▲ *Queen Victoria, in whose honour Cobh was renamed*

The Second World War

During the war years, known euphemistically in Ireland as 'the Emergency', de Valera opted for a policy of neutrality.

THIS POLICY GREATLY enhanced de Valera's status at home. More than anything, it demonstrated his country's independence, especially in relation to Britain. Despite the fact that Ireland was not officially involved in the War, however, many Irish joined British regiments and went off to fight what they saw as the tyranny of Germany. They were, indeed, well placed to understand the plight of the countries invaded by a much stronger neighbour.

The war brought much economic hardship and damaged many of the new industries that the government had been developing. Many commodities were scarce and rationing was introduced. Yet the war also helped the country's spirit, emphasising the need for self-reliance. It also helped to heal the wounds of the civil war period, as people with different political opinions often worked together to keep the country going.

◄ *Eamon de Valera in 1947*

When Winston Churchill made a point of criticising Ireland for her neutrality during the war in his victory broadcast, de Valera made an emotive response that echoed the sentiments of many Irish at the time: 'Mr Churchill is proud of Britain's stand alone, after France had fallen and before America entered the war. Could he not find in his heart the generosity to acknowledge that there is a small nation that stood alone not for one year or two, but for several hundred years against aggression; that has endured spoilations, famines, massacres in endless succession; that was clubbed many times into insensibility, but that each time on returning to consciousness took up the fight anew; a small nation that could never be got to accept defeat and has never surrendered her soul?'

Winston Churchill, leader of Britain during the Second World War ▶

Economic Growth in the 1950s-60s

In an open economy, a nation should develop a comparative advantage in some products and then be able to compete, or even dominate, internationally in the production of those products.

PROTECTIVE POLICIES prevented this from happening in Ireland. A policy of open trade in a nation with a low income *per capita*, such as Ireland, should also lead to an advantage in the production of labour-intensive products, because the cost of labour should be relatively low. In Ireland's case this never occurred because the costs of imported manufacturing inputs were too high due to tariffs, which resulted in high overall costs of production.

The tariffs, combined with poor domestic infrastructure, disrupted the efficient allocation of resources and resulted in higher costs. These realities were not only the result of protectionist economic policies previous to the period being considered here. The protectionist policies continued and some new ones were actually instituted in the post-war era. It was not until the late 1950s that the barriers to free international trade were finally dismantled.

Since then, Ireland's story has been one of steady economic progress and growth. Emigration continued to be a major problem up until recent years and agriculture remained the most important industry.

In the 1950s and 1960s, the government sponsored programmes of economic expansion. These modernised the Irish economy and paved the

Agriculture remained Ireland's most important industry ▶

way for Irish entry into the European Economic Community at the same time as Britain and Denmark in 1973.

While Britain, especially under Conservative governments has had an uneasy relationship with what is now the European Union, Ireland has wholeheartedly embraced the European ideals, something which can be most simply demonstrated by an examination of the contrasting positions taken by Ireland and Britain on the question of the single European currency.

Ireland and the International Stage

Ireland has always been keen to play its part in world affairs, its neutrality and independence being seen to give the country certain advantages in diplomatic and peacekeeping missions. Ireland was a member of the League of Nations in the 1930s, with Eamon de Valera serving as President of its Council in 1932 and of its assembly in 1938.

MEMBERS OF THE Irish parliament also worked with representatives of the Canadian government. They were instrumental in the restructuring of the British Commonwealth as an association of self-governing states and removing the stigma of empire. Since the Second World War, Ireland has played an honourable role in the United Nations Organisation, supplying peace-keeping troops for missions in the Congo, Cyprus and the Lebanon. In the 1990s, former Irish president, Mary Robinson, was appointed United Nations High Commissioner for Human Rights.

The 1990s have also seen a further surge in the Irish economy, which has been dubbed the 'Celtic

◀ *Mary Robinson*

Tiger' by commentators. Ireland, with its well-educated young workforce has been a popular choice as a European headquarters for many multinational companies including many involved in the computer and related software industries.

Ireland is noted for its many political leaders of industry. However, Irish citizens have also made a serious impact behind the scenes in many other areas. In Britain alone, an inordinate percentage of executive positions are held by those of Irish nationality or descent. Peter Sutherland was the head of the group that brought the historic GATT trade negotiations to a successful conclusion. These are the tip of the creative iceberg.

Today, the Irish Republic is a bright, buoyant place with an open and rapidly changing society. It has come a very long way since the dark days of the famine, just 150 years ago.

▼ *Ireland's future looks brighter than it has seemed for decades*

Northern Ireland Before the 1960s

Northern Ireland has had a very different history since its separation from the rest of Ireland. Its government was completely dominated by the elderly leaders of the Unionist Party.

THE UNIONISTS CHOSE to consolidate their party's dominant position and to brook no opposition from within their own ranks, never mind from others.

Sir James Craig, later Lord Craigavon, was prime minister from 1921 until his death in 1940. J. M. Andrews, his successor, had been in cabinet since 1921 and Lord Brookeborough was prime minister from 1943 to 1963.

Craig had unambiguously declared that the Northern Ireland government would be 'a Protestant parliament for a Protestant people' and partition had indeed guaranteed a

Lord Craigavon, after laying a wreath commemorating those who died in 1914–18 ▶

large in-built Protestant majority. Catholics made up about one third of the population, but with the removal of proportional representation, the Unionist Party soon came to dominate both local and central government. Where necessary, as in Derry, blatant gerrymandering was employed to ensure that there would always be a unionist-controlled council, despite the city's Catholic nationalist majority.

Despite its dominance, the Unionist Party did not rush to make sweeping changes. Instead, it claimed to offer its citizens the same rights as people living in Britain and chose to copy much of the legislation enacted in Westminster. The major exception to this was in the area of security, where a Special Powers Act was retained on the statute books and used to suppress all serious political opposition.

The 1930s saw Northern Ireland's economy severely affected by the worldwide recession, hitting the major traditional industries of

▲ *Unemployment demonstration, Cork, 1933*

ship-building, linen and agriculture particularly hard. Unemployment remained high and was at 20 per cent at the outbreak of the Second World War.

The war, which saw the deployment of American troops in many parts of Northern Ireland, boosted economic prosperity, although Belfast suffered many casualties in German air raids in 1941.

After the war, Northern Ireland began to prosper, with many new industries setting up in the province – although usually only to areas east of the river Bann: the areas that were most densely Protestant. Catholics were treated as second-class citizens, and so it is not surprising that, when they gained access to better education through the 1947 Education Act, enacted following a similar move in Westminster, they began to demand their rights.

As with civil-rights campaigns in other parts of the world, the cause for equality was not only debated on housing estates and in public houses, but also in universities; this debate was taken onto the streets. The Protestant hierarchy were affronted with the accusations being levelled at them, whether they were true or not. The cause, then, for equality was given articulation by the likes of John Hume, who taught history in a Derry college, Bernadette Devlin, Ivan Cooper and Eamonn McCann. These were people who knew Irish history inside out and were determined that, in an increasingly media-conscious world, the message would get out.

It would be wrong to suggest that Northern Ireland's wrongs began with partition. Sectarianism had been a problem in the north-east of Ireland for well over 200 years and possibly for longer. When the Orange Order was founded in 1795, it was giving a structure to something which already existed in society.

The Orange Order was an embodiment of already existing tensions in Irish society ▶

Terence O'Neill and The Troubles

Captain Terence O'Neill (1914–90) was born and educated in England; his father had been Westminster MP for mid-Antrim.

O'NEILL WAS ELECTED prime minister of Northern Ireland in 1963 after Sir Basil Brookeborough suffered a stroke. A moderate Unionist, he attempted to improve relations with the Dublin government. He met with much opposition in Northern Ireland and was undermined by members of his own party. He resigned in 1969, and soon retired to England where he died in 1990.

O'Neill oversaw the period of Irish history which would finally see the change for which the Irish had been battling for so many decades.

▲ *Barbed wire partitions, Londonderry, 1969*

With the outbreak of the Troubles at the end of the 1960s, the border became a much more obvious and ominous presence, as it became heavily militarised with border checkpoints and patrons. Many minor roads were cratered or blocked by the British security forces, creating long detours for many of the people who lived in these areas, and cutting people off from neighbours who happened to live on the other side.

The concrete and the steel also had a psychological effect, and there were many people, especially in the South, who would readily admit that before the present improvement in the northern situation and the relaxation of border controls, they had not crossed the border for many years. Many in the North tried to maintain a semblance of normality, but most could not deny that there was a change happening.

In towns like Derry, where the Catholic population had endured centuries of being downtrodden, there was a renewed confidence that times were changing. Catholic businessmen and artists were seen as being successful. Generally, the Catholic population realised that they were every bit as good as their Protestant neighbours.

▲ *Heavily armed troops, Londonderry, 1969*

The Civil Rights Movement in Ireland

In 1967, the Northern Ireland Civil Rights Association was formed. Following the example of Martin Luther King's black civil rights movement in America, they took to the streets in non-violent protest marches.

AS BEFORE, ANY CONCESSIONS granted to Catholics were seen by the Protestant majority as an attempt to undermine and overthrow their position. Subsequently, the civil rights demonstrations were aggressively attacked and broken up by the Royal Ulster Constabulary, the B-Specials and Protestant extremists.

A particular issue which had annoyed the civil rights protesters was the decision to site Northern Ireland's second university east of the Bann, near the Protestant town of Coleraine, rather than in the Catholic city of Derry, which seemed to many the obvious place.

When they came, reforms were not so much too little as too late. Unrest reached such a peak on the streets that the British army was deployed. The army was initially welcomed by the Catholics, who hoped they would be protected from Protestant mobs, who were attacking them and burning them out of their houses, especially in Belfast.

▲ *Aftermath of an explosion*

▲ *Riot police in Londonderry, 1969*

The Protestant right wing, which had been responsible for many of the disturbances, demanded that the government take stronger action against the law-breakers, knowing that they themselves would be largely exempt from the rigours of any subsequent legislation. The Northern Ireland government, now under Brian Faulkner, responded by introducing internment without trial, a measure he had used previously as Minister of Home Affairs to stifle an IRA campaign of attacks at the end of the 1950s.

Nearly 350 people were arrested, many of whom were grossly ill-treated, later successfully taking cases against the authorities to the European Court of Human Rights. Virtually all who were arrested were Catholics, while the Protestant agitators were ignored. All this caused great resentment and greatly boosted the membership of the IRA, which had largely been dormant up until 1970.

British soldier, wearing a gas mask, on the streets of Ulster ▶

The Troubles - Dark Days

An event that would have an enormous impact on Irish history would happen in the second half of the twentieth century. Once more, it was shrouded in tragedy.

I N DERRY, ON 30 January 1972, a civil rights and anti-internment march was to take place in the Catholic ghetto areas of the city, marching from the Creggan estate down into the Bogside. The official and provisional IRA branches in the city agreed to put their arms away and said they would not confront the British army.

The British army, however, had other plans, and were spoiling for a fight. The infamous parachute regiment had been brought into the city specially to deal with the march. After some stone-throwing, the army used this excuse to march into the Bogside, where protesters had been listening to speeches. Claiming that they had been shot at, the paratroopers shot back, killing a total 13 people on the day, with another dying of his wounds some time later. Ireland's second 'Bloody Sunday' caused great anger across the country and brought the magnitude of the situation to the eyes of the outside world. The repercussions were felt throughout Ireland.

Children watching the parade that turned into Bloody Sunday ▶

Brian Faulkner (1921–77) was the last prime minister of Northern Ireland, he worked in his family's shirt-making business before entering parliament as the MP for East Down in 1949.

Ten years later, he was appointed Minister for Home Affairs and, later, Minister of Commerce. He succeeded Sir James Chichester-Clarke as prime minister in 1971 and was responsible for the introduction of internment in 1971.

Direct rule from Westminster was introduced 25 March 1972. He later became head of the executive that was set up under the Sunningdale Agreement of 1974. This power sharing executive was brought down after five months by the loyalist Ulster Workers' Council strike. He retired from politics in 1976 and died the following year in a horse-riding accident.

The UWC strike also brought the situation in Northern Ireland to the point of no return. It was final proof, as if proof were needed, that Northern Ireland as then constituted, was a failure. Two months after Northern Ireland was brought to its knees by the strike, the British government suspended the Northern

Brian Faulkner, photographed in 1972 ▶

Ireland government and parliament, introducing direct rule from Westminster. 467 people died in political and sectarian violence in Northern Ireland in 1972, the worst year of the Troubles – a further sign of the hopelessness of the situation.

During the 1970s and 1980s, several attempts were made to bring politicians together in an effort to find a solution. These efforts all ended in failure. The British government lapsed into a policy of containment for the most part, although Margaret Thatcher as prime minister was keen to openly confront the IRA, especially in 1981 during the republican hunger strikes.

Ten men, including Bobby Sands, who had been elected MP for Fermanagh-South Tyrone, died in prison. As the 1980s continued, the situation seemed very bleak, with no apparent hope of any progress towards a resolution of the various conflicts.

▲ *Bertie Ahern (left), US Senator George Mitchell (centre) and Tony Blair (right) shake hands, 1998*

HOPE FOR THE FUTURE

IT WAS ONLY WHEN TALKS began between John Hume, leader of the nationalist Social Democratic and Labour Party (SDLP), and Gerry Adams, president of Sinn Fein, that new options and possibilities began to be explored. These contacts eventually led to the Downing Street Declaration, signed by British prime minister, John Major and Taoiseach Albert Reynolds in 1993, followed by cease-fires from the main paramilitary groups the following year.

Progress since then has at times been frustratingly slow and there have been major setbacks. However, the demilitarisation of the situation by all sides has brought an air of normality and calm back to the streets. While the political process continues, there is hope that the ideas outlined in the Good Friday Agreement of 1998 can be built upon in the not too distant future.

▲ *Copies of the Agreement signed by all parties at the Stormont peace talks*

Glossary

VERNACULAR LITERATURES
Traditional Irish literature that is written in Irish Gaelic or in dialect.

MESOLITHIC PEOPLE
These middle stone age people inhabited Ireland from about 9000 BC to 3000 BC. The period is characterised by the microliths that remain throughout Ireland.

MICROLITHS
These mesolithic tools were made by inserting flint blades into wood in rows.

GRAVEGOODS
Gravegoods were left in Celtic burial tombs reflect the status of the deceased. They were often made of bronze.

PASSAGE GRAVE
The Irish Neolithic peoples constructed these graves around 5000 years ago. They consisted of a long stone-roofed entrance passage leading into a stone tomb.

NEOLITHIC
Or New Stone Age, was a period that began in Ireland around 3000 BC and lasted until about 2400 BC. It was characterised by early agricultural communities and megalithic tombs.

DRUID
Celtic for 'Knowing the Old Oak Tree'. These priests, teachers and judges were members of the learned class in Celtic Ireland from around 300 BC until the arrival of Christianity around 500 AD.

PAGAN
A member of a Pre-Christian religion in Ireland.

HIBERNO
Romanesque architecture – This style of architecture developed in the eleventh and twelfth centuries and was the Irish interpretation of the contemporary European trend to return to the Roman ideal.

HUGUENOT

A follower of, or relating to, the French Protestant Church in the sixteenth and seventeenth centuries.

SYNOD

An ecclesiastical council convened to discuss church affairs in Ireland.

KEEP

The main and often the most strongly fortified tower found within the walls of a medieval castle.

BLACK DEATH

The plague affected Ireland from 1348-49, in which time it changed the country's demography, economy and its relations with Britain.

PLANTAGENET DYNASTY

This royal house of England reigned from 1154-1485. By the late fourteenth century the dynasty was divided as the two houses, York and Lancaster,

fought in the War of the Roses for the succession to the throne.

LANCASTRIANS

The supporters of the House of Lancaster fought for the sons of Edward III in the War of the Roses. The Lancastrian pretender, Henry Tudor, ended the war in 1485 by defeating the Yorkist king Richard III.

YORKISTS

The supporters of the Plantagenet House of York were defeated in the War of the Roses in 1485. See Lancastrians.

SPANISH NETHERLANDS

Present day Belgium and Luxembourg were Spanish provinces from c.1579-1713.

TENANT FARMERS

Made up the majority of Catholic farmers, in 1778 only 5% of Catholics owned land. Landlords were predominately protestant and absent.

ORANGE ORDER

Established in 1795 by protestants from the Peep O'Day Boys group, their aim was to defend their own position against the Catholics and anti-Catholic legislation.

TEMPERANCE MOVEMENT

Founded in 1838 by Father Theobold Matthews in an attempt to end the problem of alcohol abuse in Ireland.

FENIANS

The American wing of the Irish Republican Brotherhood was a secret Catholic society founded in 1858 by John O'Mahony dedicated to armed revolution.

SMALL FARMERS

Unlike tenant farmers these owned their own small parcel of land but they continued to suffer economically and from the threat of famine throughout the nineteenth century.

LOCK OUT

As a response to the 1913 general strikes, Dublin industrialists instituted a lockout against union members.

LA TÈNE HEARTLAND

An area of present day Switzerland on Lake Neuchâtel where an advanced Celtic civilisation developed from the

mid fifth century BC until
c.500 BC.

WAGON BURIALS

These immensely
rich Celtic
burials were a
formal
expression of
the status of
the deceased.
Within the
central grave a
wagon was placed next to
the bed which would have
been decorated.

CONVENANTERS

These extreme Presbyterians raised
armies against King Charles in the
seventeenth century in order to
defend their doctrine of extreme
absolutism.

ROYALISTS

The Royalists supported Charles I
against Cromwell and his
followers, known as the
Roundheads.

Author Biography

Séamas Mac Annaidh

Séamas Mac Annaidh is a full-time writer and broadcaster, who is especially interested in local history and genealogy. His works include numerous articles and lectures, four novels, a translation of an Italian novel and a collection of short stories. His hobbies include travelling, hill-walking and music of all kinds. His wife, Joy Beatty, is a viola player.

Picture Credits

Bill Doyle: 45, 57, 61, 63, 64-65, 97, 126, 141, 165, 211, 225, 248, 275.

Christie's Images: 23, 26, 115, 123, 135, 151.

David Lyons/Event Horizons: 14-15, 16, 17, 21, 27, 33, 54, 71, 95, 131, 313.

Edimedia: 79, 82, 112, 121, 154, 176, 216, 220, 221, 233, 245, 259, 267.

Foundry Arts: 48, 172, 261, 264, 277, 289.

Image Select: 36, 72, 92, 99, 132, 137, 146, 209, 226, 237, 274. **Image Select/Giraudon:** 6, 42, 91, 107, 136. **Image Select/Ann Ronan:** 67, 69, 153, 162, 163, 181, 184, 187, 188, 196, 198, 199, 232, 268, 278, 293, 311.

Mary Evans: 7, 9, 19, 20, 28, 30 (t), 31, 35, 38, 47, 51, 55, 56, 59, 60, 68, 73, 74, 76, 77, 78, 83, 89, 90, 94, 101, 103, 111, 119, 120, 122, 138, 140, 142, 143, 147, 150, 156, 158-159, 160, 161, 166, 167, 168, 170, 173, 174, 177, 178, 179, 180, 182, 183, 186, 189, 191, 192, 193, 194, 195, 197, 200, 201, 202, 212, 215, 216, 217, 218, 219, 223, 231, 234, 241, 243, 246, 250, 253, 269, 273, 272, 280, 281, 283, 285, 286, 291.

Michael Diggin: 24, 25, 37, 52-53, 70, 86, 104, 116-117, 124, 127, 133, 155, 169, 185, 206, 207, 208, 222, 239, 288.

Still Moving Picture Co.: Michael Brooke 34. Still Moving Picture Co./Scottish Tourist Board: 39,

Topham: 8, 10, 13, 18, 43, 49, 58, 75, 81, 85, 88, 96, 98, 108, 110, 113, 118, 125, 136, 147, 148, 149, 157, 171, 203, 204, 205, 206, 213, 214, 224, 227, 235, 240, 247, 248, 251, 252, 254, 255, 256, 257, 258, 265, 269, 270, 271, 279, 282, 287, 290, 292, 295, 296, 297, 298, 299, 301, 302, 303, 304, 305, 306, 307, 308, 309.

Trinity College, Dublin: 93, 175.

Visual Arts Library: 22. **Visual Arts Library /Artephot** 29, 30 (b), 139. **Visual Arts Library /Trinity College, Dublin** 40, 129.

Index

O'Connors 50, 55, 57, 58, 64-5, 91
O'Donnell, Red Hugh 96, 97, 98
O'Donnell, Rory 100
O'Donovan Rossa, Jeremiah 179, 237
O'Duffy, Eoin 287
ogham 26-7
O'Higgins, Kevin 283, 286
Oiche na Gaoithe Moire 156-7
Oisin 31-2
O'Mahoney, John 178-9
O'Maille, Earnan 281
O'Moores 91
One Hundred Years War 68
O'Neill, Shane 90, 95
O'Neill, Brian 65
O'Neill, Conn 90
O'Neill, Hugh 92, 96-7, 98, 100
O'Neill, Owen Roe 108, 109, 112
O'Neill, Sir Phelim 107, 108
O'Neill, Terence 302-3
O'Neill, Turlough Luineach 96
Orange Card 198
Orange Lodges 135
Orange Order 134-5, 147, 213, 300
Orangemen 120, 140, 147, 192
O'Rourke 54, 55, 57
O'Shea, Captain 200
O'Shea, Katherine 200
O'Shea, Paudie 205
Ostmen see Vikings
outdoor relief 160

P

paganism 30, 31-2
Parachute Regiment 306
Parnell, Charles Stewart 187, 188-9, 190, 193, 194, 199, 200-1
partition 214, 262, 274, 5, 298
Partridge, William 226
Patrick, St. 19, 28-30, 32
Pearse, Patrick H. 232, 233, 234-7, 242, 243, 247
Pearse, William 236
Peep o' Day Boys 131, 135
Penal Laws 123-4, 137, 152
Philip II, King of Spain 91, 94, 98
Phoenix National and Literary Society 179
Phoenix Park Murders 194-5

phythphthora infestans 166
Pilgrimage of Grace 88
Pilltown 76
piping 207
Pitt, William 144-5
Plantagenet dynasty 74
Plantation of Ulster 100, 102-3
Plunkett, Joseph 232, 243
Plunkett, Philomena 232
Plunkett, Sir Oliver 116-17
poetry 207
poets 11, 37, 128
police force 287, 288
Poor Law 160-1
population 12, 168
potatoe blight 166
poteen 162
poverty 126, 168
Poynings Law 80, 137
Poynings, Sir Edward 80
Presbyterians 132, 151
Presidents 290
Pretenders, The 78-9
Proclamation of the Provisional Government of the Irish Republic 242-3
Protestantism 102, 126-7, 184-5, 213
Protestants 89, 100, 115, 123, 131, 132-3, 150-1, 198, 304-5
provinces 25, 92
Public Safety Bill 286-7
public work schemes 167
Purchase of Land Act (1885) 195
Pym, John 110

Q

Quakers 167

R

Radio Eireann 289
Raleigh, Walter 94
Rathcormac, massacre of 157
Rathlin Island 94
Rathmullen 100
rebellions 106-7, 140-1, 142-3
see also Easter Rising; Emmet's Rising
recession 299-300
Redmond, John 212-13, 216, 219, 227, 229, 231, 251, 253
Reformation 89

Reformed Presbyterian Church 184
religion, freedom of 289
Repeal Association 174, 181
retribution, Cromwell's 114-15
Reynolds, Albert 309
Richard, Duke of York 75, 79
Richard II 66, 69, 72-3, 74
Richard III 74, 75
Robinson, Mary 296
Rollo 52
Romans 6
Roundheads 111
Royal Ulster Constabulary 304
Ryan, Mrs 158
Ryder, Reverend Archdeacon 158

S

St Canice's Cathedral 63
St Clair-sur-Epte 52
St Enda's 236
St Mary's Cathedral 34-5, 63
St Patrick's Cathedral 44, 63
St Peters Church 117
Sainte Colombe 23
Salisbury, Lord 199
Sands, Bobby 308
Sarah 172
Sarsfield, Patrick 122
Schomberg, General 120
Scots Gaelic 24, 25
Scottish mercenaries 64
Scottish settlers 103
Second Home Rule Bill 202-3
Second World War 287, 292-3, 300
secret societies 150
sectarianism 198, 300
security forces 303
separatism 202-3
Shaftesbury, Lord 116
shamrock 32
Shannon Scheme 289
Sheehy, Mike 205
sieges
of Derry 118-19
of Limerick 122-3
Silken Thomas 84-5
Simnel, Lambert 78-9, 80
Sinn Fein 211, 252-3, 261, 274, 288
Skeffington, Sir William 84

Index